TAKING THE LEAD

TAKING THE LEAD

Lessons from a Life in Motion

Derek Hough

wm

WILLIAM MORROW

An Imprint of HarperCollins*Publishers*

HarperCollins books may be purchased for educational, business, or sales promotional use. For information please e-mail the Special Markets Department at SPsales@harpercollins.com.

FIRST EDITION

Designed by Lisa Stokes

Library of Congress Cataloging-in-Publication Data has been applied for.

ISBN 978-0-06-232319-4

14 15 16 17 18   ov/rrd   10 9 8 7 6 5 4 3 2 1

To all the people who have inspired, challenged, and supported me in my life. Thank you for your love and encouragement. You always remind me to believe in myself—the person I am and the person I want to be.

CONTENTS

FOREWORD

I AM SO BLESSED to have gotten to know Derek, and honored that he asked me to write the foreword for his book. He's the most amazing person—not just a choreographer, dancer, and teacher, but an amazing human being. Spending so much quality time together confined in a dance studio when we did *Dancing with the Stars* Season 16, I really got to know him well. I cherish his friendship, and I admire him so much for his work ethic.

From the first time we met, I could see he was very passionate, and he brings that passion to everything he does. That resonates with the audiences both live and watching on TV at home. People build their entire schedules around being able to tune in and see Derek dance. I know I do! Millions have fallen in love with him, and it's easy for me to understand why. He's so generous with his heart and his spirit. Even if you don't know him, you feel you can walk up to him on the street and strike up a conversation: "Hi, man! I'm a fan." I will never forget how he would race out into the audience and pull people out onto the dance floor with him during our commercial breaks.

The audience at home never sees this, but I got a front-row view. One time, there was this elderly lady in a wheelchair, and she told him that her greatest dream was to dance with him. So what did Derek do? He rolled her right out onto that stage and twirled her around. He gave her the dance of her life. She was so happy, you'd think Elvis had come back!

But that's Derek. He's a giver and he never stops giving. He's a perfectionist, yes, but it's because he wants you to be the best you can be. He never criticizes in a way that's harsh or knocks you down. Instead, his corrections were building me up, week by week. That's a great gift that he has: to see the strengths in someone and bring them out. He saw things in me I didn't even know I was capable of. He never once showed up to a rehearsal with a prechoreographed routine. He built each dance around me—what I could do, and what he knew I *would* be able to do with a little practice. How many pep talks did he give me before we went out onstage? I know I would have been lost without him.

I'm so not surprised he wrote this book, because he's all about inspiring and connecting with people. He is the most incredible motivator. My biggest fear doing *Dancing with the Stars* was disappointing him. In rehearsals, he'd seen me at my absolute best and my absolute worst. The audience hadn't. He'd know if I gave it my all or not. I wanted so badly to give a great performance and make him proud.

He taught me so many things, but the ones that stick out are the lessons about getting out there and *doing*. I had huge anxiety when we first started, and he helped me wipe that word from my vocabulary. He gave my anxiety a name—Anxious Annie—and he told me I couldn't play with her anymore! He also taught me how important it is to keep moving, and to maintain even today the same mobility I had when I was dancing. When I move, it's going to help me both physically and mentally. And if I'm able to, there's no excuse not to, except that I'm being lazy.

I think whatever the future holds for Derek, he will always be a part of something meaningful and that matters. There's a big difference between being alive and living—and he's the type of person who believes if you're alive, then you should live to your fullest. I know that there is so much more he will bring to this world—and I can't wait to see it.

—KELLIE PICKLER

TAKING THE LEAD

INTRODUCTION

I'M USED TO leading on the dance floor. The music starts, and I take my partner's hand, guiding her into position, controlling the flow of energy, directing the movement.

But when it comes to life, taking the lead isn't so simple. It takes guts, but not the kind needed to jump out of an airplane from fourteen thousand feet or perform live in front of an audience of millions. Trust me, I've done both. It's having the courage required to uncover the bigger picture. Where are you going and how will you get there? And most important, who will you become on your journey? Every mistake, every twist, turn, or total wipeout hands you an opportunity to learn and grow. Are you brave enough to take it?

I wasn't. Honestly, the idea of writing a book about my life scared the hell out of me. I didn't think I was ready to go there. It felt overwhelming—a lot of memories tangled up in emotions. I wasn't sure the timing was right (I was competing in Seasons 17 and 18 of *Dancing with the Stars*) and I wasn't convinced I knew what to say or how to say it. So I did what I do whenever I'm stuck on a dance and I don't have a clue how to choreograph it. I break it down. I look at it, not as a whole, but as a series of steps that come together. Somehow, seeing each phase of my life this way brought it all into focus. The lessons became clear, the experiences came flooding back in vivid detail, and I felt empowered.

I think I've just begun stepping up and owning my life, and I have a long way to go and lots of things I want and need to accomplish. But at least I'm headed in the right direction. I've started seeing my journey as a work in progress—sometimes I've rocked it, sometimes I've stumbled or tripped over my own feet. But every move I've made has shaped me into the person I am today. I believe life isn't about finding yourself, but creating yourself. My friend Tony Robbins asks, "What if life isn't happening to us? What if it is happening *for* us?" I believe that when you seize control, you're nobody's doormat or punching bag anymore—not even you can stand in your own way (and I am harder on myself than anyone else is). You open yourself up to endless possibilities.

Not many people know that I was bullied as a kid. By bullied, I don't mean teased or picked on or called names. I mean terrorized for a long time. I stayed silent until now—not even my parents knew the extent of the physical and emotional abuse I suffered. When I shared my story with them, they were shocked and saddened. Why didn't I come to them? Why didn't I ask for help? Truthfully? I was paralyzed. Even as a grown man, I find these memories hard to revisit. But I see now that taking the lead means reclaiming who you are and taking back your true self. It's taking off the blinders and letting go of whatever is holding you back. It's embracing the moment for what it is and for what it teaches you. It's putting the past behind you and clearing a new path for the future. I can't change what happened, but I can change the meaning of it and how I look at it.

Fear is a great motivator. I tell that to my partners on *Dancing with the Stars* all the time. Go on, be scared. Get out of your comfort zone. Align yourself with your fear and use it to propel you to progress. Look your demons in the eye and kick 'em to the curb. For Kellie Pickler, it was learning to get out of her own way. For Ricki Lake, it was finding something she loved in the mirror. For Maria Menounos, it was dancing through the pain of injury to discover an inner strength she never knew she had. For Jennie Garth, it was her first perfect score and knowing nothing could hold her back anymore. For Amber Riley, it was truly believing in her own greatness. Each and every one of these ladies took the lead in their lives. Mirror Ball or no Mirror Ball, in my eyes, they're all winners.

Looking back on my life up to this point (because believe me, I've got a lot of living left to do!), it's been quite a trip. I'm not the skinny, awkward little boy from Salt Lake City anymore. I'm happy with the man I've become, and I owe a great deal to the people who have influenced me and inspired me along the way. These have been my friends, family, coaches, and mentors, the ones who pushed me to push myself. They've even been my rivals—the dancers who were so good, they made me want to be better. Every obstacle has been a reason to keep moving forward. Paring this book down to the most important moments in my life was no easy task—I could write ten books, not just one, of everything I've experienced! But these are the experiences that resonate with me the most: the ones that have made me stop, take stock, appreciate, and affirm the person I want to be.

I hope in reading my stories you discover or rediscover who you are and learn how to take the lead in your own life. I hope you learn to channel your passion, harness your power, and connect with your joy. Joseph Campbell, the American mythologist, lecturer, and writer, believed you should "follow your bliss." This is what I do and what I've always tried to do. Life is a dance, but it's much more than mastering the steps. It's pushing your boundaries, shattering your limits, and exploding in a breathtaking burst of light.

REFLECTING ON DEREK

"Derek Hough is magic. You can see it in the way he dances, the way he speaks, and the way he brings out the very best in others. He is a true leader and I am inspired whenever I am in his presence."

—TONY ROBBINS

1

INDIANA JONES AND THE
BROTHERS DOWN THE BLOCK

I AM A FIRM believer that you are the sum of your parts—which is why my family history is important to me. People are always asking me if my dancing ability comes from nature or nurture. I think it's both; I've killed myself training over the years, and I have the bumps, bruises, and bulging vertebrae to prove it. But I must admit that there is dance DNA pumping through these veins.

My dad was born in Coeur d'Alene, Idaho, and his mom, Grandma Coke (her real name is Colleen, but she was nicknamed for her love of hot cocoa), taught dance for her church youth group. My granddad, "Bubble Head Bob Hough," was a rock and roll deejay—so he would book record hops and spin the tunes kids danced to. My mom's parents, Dawn and Romaine, worked as dance teachers in Idaho Falls, Utah, for a short while.

My parents' first date took place on a dance floor (the irony of this doesn't escape me). It was a school winter social at Ricks College at Brigham Young University. Dad had some pretty smooth moves—or at least he thought he did! He joined the ballroom dance team, not because he loved to cha-cha, but basically because he heard there were good-looking girls in the club. That's where he and Mom met. They were never actually partners, but Dad always had his eye on Marianne, the pretty fraternity "Dream Girl" (a title she won in a pageantlike competition). He kept asking her out and trying to walk her to class, and as many times as she politely said no (she had a boyfriend serving a Latter-Day Saints mission and was doing her best to stay loyal), he always asked again. He finally wore her down with his relentlessness. His friends didn't nickname him "Bold Bruce" for nothing!

Things moved pretty quickly from that point on. They dated for four months and were engaged in June. They got married two months later, on August 19, 1976. My mom had my sister Sharee when she was barely twenty—no more than a kid herself. But she could handle it. She was the only girl in a family with three brothers and she prided herself on being tough. Both my mom and dad were raised Mormon, and they brought us up *very* Mormon. We went to church every Sunday and fasted once a month. There was absolutely no swearing allowed in our home. If I let out a cuss, I'd get my mouth washed out with soap. At Christmas, we brought meals to the needy, and before every dinner, we said grace. At night, I would kneel down at my bedside and pray. I'm not sure if I understood what our faith was all about back then—my prayers were mostly things that I had memorized and recited, and I would say the words without knowing their meanings. Nonetheless, my parents insisted that religion be part of our daily lives.

This didn't stop us, however, from being a pretty wild family. We were faithful, respectful, and ritualistic—but we could also explode into craziness whenever music started playing. Any time Bruce Springsteen, Bob Seger, or Billy Joel came on the radio, my sisters and I would start dancing around the kitchen, knocking plates and glasses off the shelves. My friends used to tease me about how much I loved oldies music. Truthfully, it reminded me of my grandparents' houseboat and the times we spent there in the summers. Those were my glory days. We would have huge family reunions there with my dad's side of the family—all my aunts, uncles, and cousins. At times, there were thirty of us there having a huge party on the lake. We drove twelve hours to reach the boat—my parents, my sisters, and I all stuffed into a red van with a crummy, old portable TV lodged between the passenger and driver's sides. We'd watch movies driving up and listen to U2's *Joshua Tree*. Its songs became the anthems of my childhood.

When we arrived at the houseboat, my dad became a different person—someone I barely recognized but loved to hang with. He worked in radio and later started a satellite communications company, so he was often traveling for work. But when he arrived at the houseboat, he was transformed. He cut loose, sang karaoke, acted like a complete dork. I'd sit there watching him and think to myself, Who is this man?

My mom's job was raising us. She cooked, cleaned, and kept us entertained. I don't think any of us made her life particularly easy—there were five kids in all: my three older sisters, Sharee, Marabeth, and Katherine; then me and Julianne. Sharee had a very strong personality and was opinionated about everything, probably because she was the oldest and wisest (or at least she thought so!). Marabeth was quiet, and Katherine had a wild sense of humor. We used to call her Lucille Ball because she was always cracking us up. When I picture my older sisters as teenagers, they were the funniest eighties stereotypes: big, curled hair and neon wristbands and headbands. I fell toward the middle of the Hough pack, and you know the reputation middle children have: always trying to get attention, always making mischief. That was me, big time. I remember constantly jumping around, leaping off the furniture like it was my personal jungle gym. We have dozens of videos of me dancing around the living room and ricocheting off the walls like a pinball.

They teach you in church that idle hands are the devil's workshop. I don't know about that, but I do know that I always had the feeling that I needed to be *doing*. My mom referred to it as ants in my pants, but it was more than that. I just couldn't sit still. I worried something important would pass me by if I did, and my imagination never allowed me downtime. I suffered from major FOMO: fear of missing out.

My sisters and I were always making movies and commercials with a camcorder. The slow-motion button intrigued me—I loved to watch myself suspended in midair. I would crank up the music from *Mortal Kombat* and do a running front flip off my bed. I studied the playback: What if I put in a bit more torque or a little more rotation? Would it make me fly higher? Would I stay in the air a few minutes longer? I was very scientific about it. Even though I hated science class in school, the physics of the perfect flip fascinated me. I wanted to be a Ninja Turtle.

I felt like there were kids around me who were much more physical and could do more than me, so I'd try and figure out how they did it. My imagination was on the entire time; I never hit the off button. It felt as if I were living in a movie: from the moment I woke up I could hear the soundtrack in my head, and I assumed different characters. My sisters and I would re-create scenes from movies that we loved, like *Labyrinth* or *Legend*—all the mystical fantasy stuff.

My mom let us have our fun, and she had the patience of a saint with me. No matter where I was, I wound up in trouble—or the emergency room. One time, I was at a playground, racing up and down a metal slide. I was with my cousins on the top of the slide and I called to her, "Ma, watch me! Watch me!" I wanted her to see me barrel down on my stomach. She wasn't paying attention, and my cousin was losing patience and wanted her turn. So she pushed me. I remember it all in slow motion, and I'm not sure when I blacked out. I fell sideways down the slide, and I remember the pain of my head smashing into a metal bar. There was a lot of blood and my mother screaming. I remember getting stitches in the emergency room and fading in and out of consciousness.

For years, I made a joke about it. If a teacher scolded me for not getting an answer quickly enough in class, I would just shrug and say, "Well, what can I tell you? A piece of my brain must have fallen out of my head when I cracked it open—it's not my fault!" A bishop, one of our local church leaders, once came over to our house and told my mother, "Your job is to keep that boy alive." He wasn't wrong. In retrospect, I was probably hyperactive, but no one formally diagnosed me. I think Mom had her suspicions, and she took matters into her own hands.

She knew that she had to keep me busy. She got me a drum set one Christmas and signed me up immediately for lessons. Every day I had another activity: baseball, soccer, karate, even art classes. Sometimes, she'd have to drag me kicking and screaming to them—I never wanted to stop playing for something as trivial as karate class. I'd pout all the way in the car, but once I was there and into it, I was glad I'd come. My mom knew it might be a fight, but she had to find ways to channel all of my energy and hyperactivity into positive outlets. I give her credit—I was never bored. She even went out and got me a newspaper route. She has refused to see my hyperactivity as a disorder, so I don't either. I see it as an advantage. If your mind is always running, all you have to do is train your body to keep up with it.

Because I was the only boy, I was the only one who had his own room. It was at the top of the stairs to the left, right next to my parents' room (I suppose they put me there to keep an eye on me). My four sisters had to share two rooms to the right, while I got my own space with two single beds. Sometimes I'd get up in the middle of the night and switch beds just for fun. I could open my window and climb out on the first-story roof and lie there, gazing up at the night sky. In Boy Scouts, I learned about constellations, so I'd try to spot the

Big Dipper, Cassiopeia, the Pleiades or Seven Virgins. They seemed so far away, yet I could close one eye and balance them on the tips of my fingers.

I covered the walls of my room with pictures of tigers. I was obsessed with these beautiful, ferocious animals. My dad hoarded hundreds of *National Geographic* magazines, so one day I went through his stacks and cut out all the tiger photos I could find to make a giant collage. I don't think he was too thrilled that I tore up his collection, but he understood my passion. Tigers fascinated me for so many reasons. They're strong and fierce, but also beautiful and elegant. I remember loving the way they moved, how they were able to control their power. I would spend hours staring at their faces and drawing them: the eyes could display such a range of emotion. I loved that they have no fear. When they walk through a jungle, they own it.

Maybe I wasn't the most "normal" kid, but in our home, we were taught to embrace individuality and creativity. We didn't have a lot of toys, and for a long time I assumed we were poor. But that really wasn't the case. We could have afforded anything that the rest of the kids in our neighborhood had. My mom just thought it would be better if we used our imaginations and our hands to create things rather than buy them. I remember how badly I wanted a sword to play with. My mother handed me a piece of paper. "Draw it," she said.

So I did. I sketched out every detail, from the curve of the blade to the shiny silver handle. We had this carpenter's saw we kept in the basement, so my mom could actually cut shapes out of wood. Together, we worked to bring that sword to life. I even covered it with glow-in-the-dark paint. I thought it was pretty awesome, till I went to my friend's house and he had the Nerf 3000 thunderbolt lightning super-duper state-of-the-art lights, bells, and buzzers sword—or whatever it was called. That thing was insane! Embarrassed, I hid my makeshift sword behind my back. But looking back, I can see now the value of what my parents were trying to teach us. They were giving us the power to create, the power to see something in your mind and make it real. The lesson was probably lost on a six-year-old, but it did stick with me. Now I'm kind of like MacGyver when something needs to get done.

The Houghs were different, that's for sure, but I was never embarrassed by that fact. I was glad to be on that side of the fence. South Jordan, Utah, where we settled, was a tight community. Everyone knew everyone, and everyone knew everyone's business. We lived in a big gray house, the last one in a cul-de-sac, perched on top of a hill. We had maybe an acre of land, mostly forest, surrounding us. I would sit out in the backyard, looking out from the top of that hill, pretending I was Indiana Jones. The mountains in the distance held the promise of adventure and danger. One group of trees formed the shape of a spade, and—like a secret spot on a treasure map—I was confident that a Temple of Doom was buried there. One day, I told myself, I'd hike out there with my backpack and hat and discover it. I wanted to be in the center of danger, to go places people had never gone before. For a scrawny little kid, I had a lot of guts—either that or stupidity.

In the meantime, I had my backyard to tide me over. I would crawl on my stomach through the mud and the dirt. I'd dig trenches and build forts and wield my sword and whip as I made my way through the dark and dangerous forest filled with snakes and ancient curses. As I got a little older, I realized archeology wasn't as cool as the Indy movies made it out to be. I'd have to go to college and study a lot of boring history instead of tracking down the Lost Ark. So I abandoned that career goal. But I'm still an adventure junkie. I feel so alive when I'm on the edge—always have, always will.

Though I loved danger, I preferred to choose it myself, not have it thrust upon me. We had these neighbors down the road who clearly had something against us, although I couldn't tell you why. Their sons were big kids who were several years older than I was—and it felt like they made it their mission to torture and torment my family. If I close my eyes today, I can't see their faces; I think I blocked them out. But what I do recall vividly are feelings—how the hair on the back of my neck stood on edge whenever they came around. I remember the fear and the anxiety. I never quite knew how far they'd go or what they were capable of, so I assumed the worst. I assumed that one day, whether on purpose or by accident, they would kill me.

I wasn't that far off. Taunts and teasing and dares of "Go ahead, make me!" quickly turned physical. One of the brothers ripped my sister Sharee's earrings out of her ears, severing her lobes. She came running home with blood pouring down her neck. My mother went over to their house and went ballistic. I had never heard her scream like that before, and I probably never will again. She was a mama cub protecting her young. They insisted it was "an accident" and their mother went along with it. They were playing a game and threw a blanket over Sharee's head and snatched it away; the earrings simply caught in the fabric. But my mother made it pretty clear that they'd better stay far away from any of us or she'd take matters into her own hands (and it wouldn't be "an accident.").

Of course, this didn't stop them. One day, shortly after, it was my turn. I was about six years old, playing on a trampoline in a friend's backyard. The brothers strolled up to us and asked if we wanted to play guns. I didn't like the sound of that and hesitated, but my friend wanted to join in the fun. Before I could say anything more, the brothers dragged me off the trampoline and threw me down on the ground. One of them sat on top of me while the other tied a rope tightly around my ankles. My friend went along with it—or he was too scared to try to stop them. The ropes dug into my skin. I couldn't wriggle out of them; the knots were so tight, they cut off the circulation, and all I could feel was pins and needles in my toes. They dragged me facedown on the ground. I must have hit my head, because I tasted blood in my mouth.

They threw the other side of the rope over a thick tree branch and pulled it until I was suspended upside down by my ankles about six feet in the air. I remember feeling cold—it was dusk and there was an early autumn breeze in the air. I'm not sure how long I was in this position, only that the sun eventually set and it became pitch dark and bone-chillingly cold. I thought my head was going to explode from the blood rushing to it—or that some wild animal would discover me in the darkness and pick the flesh off my bones.

"Let me go!" I screamed. As I hung there, helpless and terrified, they spit in my face, over and over again. Then they held a pistol to my head and threatened to pull the trigger. "Shut up or we'll shoot." I knew the family hunted, so I wasn't 100 percent sure it was a toy gun. I thought I was going to die; they would leave me there to rot and freeze to death. My mom and dad or my sisters would find my body in the morning. So I screamed. I cried. I pleaded. I begged. Eventually— because I think they got tired of me carrying on—they let me down. My head was throbbing and I couldn't feel my feet. I was so cold, my teeth were chattering. I stumbled home as fast as I could, ran upstairs to my bedroom, and hid under the covers. I didn't tell anyone. I was afraid if I told, my parents would want to keep me safe, and they'd never allow me to go back out and play with my friends again. So I never told a soul.

But often, in the middle of the night, I'd wake up screaming from a nightmare. I'd dream that the brothers had strung me up again—or they were following me, guns in hand, planning their next ambush. It was the first time in my life I felt real fear, real danger. Not the kind of fear a little kid experiences when he thinks the bogeyman is lurking under his bed at night, but real fear that shakes you to your core because it's so real and so close—in my case, three houses away.

The day after the gun incident, we all went to church and I saw our neighbors there, blessing the sacrament. I was confused and angry. Didn't God see what they did to me? Didn't he care? I knew what my dad would say: "God knows and sees all. It's in his hands." But that didn't make me feel any better or less frightened that the brothers could get away with this and there would be no punishment. Looking back, it was probably the first time I questioned my faith but it wouldn't be the last. We ended up moving about three miles away a few years later, largely because of this family.

At my new school, Monte Vista, I was awkward and had a hard time making friends and trusting people. I struggled in class. Facts and figures didn't interest me. What can I say? We all learn things differently. Einstein had this theory that everyone is a genius, but if you have a classroom filled with different animals—say, a tiger, a monkey, and a fish in a bowl—and you ask them all to climb a tree, the fish is going to feel dumb because he can't climb those branches. I was the fish. But each person has their own genius and their own skill; just because you don't pass the test, it doesn't mean you're dumb. My teachers, though, constantly told me that I wasn't very smart, and after a while, I started to believe them.

Recess was the time to prove yourself. We'd play football, and because I was the runt and the new kid, I was always the last kid picked. But I'd make a very conscious decision to intercept the ball so all the cool kids would see me and notice me. Eventually, I went from being last pick to first pick. For the first time, I felt my value and my worth on a team. I had something to contribute.

Yet I never felt like I belonged at school. No one got me or shared my creativity. I was labeled "weird," so that's how I felt. No matter how I tried to act, dress, even swear like everyone else, I stuck out. Then one day, my mom dragged me to my sisters' dance classes at Center Stage Studio in Orem, Utah. My mom was always my biggest supporter, but truthfully, this was also a case of making her life easier. If all the Hough kids could go to the same after-school activity, it meant less running around for her. And Center Stage was delighted to have us all—they thought they had found themselves the blond Osmonds! When I finally stopped bitching, I realized this place was pretty magical. Everyone was so positive, so full of passion and energy. I learned a valuable lesson: You are who you hang around with.

From day 1, I had a natural rhythm and musicality. I went from the kid classes into the adult ones in a matter of weeks. I'm not sure where it came from—maybe the drum lessons my parents gave me. What I lacked in discipline and technique, I made up for with exuberance. I could actually *feel* the song rising up through my body. I could bring it to life through movement. I could express every emotion I was feeling: fear, pain, anger, frustration, loneliness, excitement. It exploded out of me. And truth be told, I was into girls, and the dance studio was *filled* with them.

So the kid who pitched a fit about going to dance class suddenly became a regular. Flying around the room, leaping through the air, I felt there was nothing—and no one—that could hold me down.

LEADING LESSONS

For a kid who never liked to pick apart a math equation, I have a pretty analytical brain. A few years ago, I came to the conclusion that you have to be an active participant in your life. You have to stop, take stock, and put things in perspective so you can see the bigger picture. I can't tell you the exact moment this truth dawned on me; there was no single earth-shattering event or catalyst. But I do remember being at a U2 concert with my sister and tearing up as all these memories of my childhood and listening to U2 flooded over me. It took me back to a time of family and fun and feeling connected. A few weeks later, I was sitting at home in my apartment, looking at my collection of trophies and thinking, Yeah? So? Now what? Winning—the one thing that used to mean the world to me—felt empty. It didn't matter how much hardware I accumulated, it didn't give me that adrenaline high anymore.

What did was the feeling of connecting with people. Not just my dance partners, but strangers who would come up to me on the street and share their stories. There have been many who cornered me in a parking lot or sent me a message on Facebook, Instagram, or Twitter. Too many to count, but one in particular stands out. A woman stopped me on the street to tell me about her grandmother. "She loved you," she said. "She watched you from her hospital bed every night *Dancing with the Stars* was on. You took her back to a time when she loved to dance. You gave her such joy in her final days." I got a lump in my throat. I had done this for someone? I thanked her and she took my hand. "No. Thank *you*." It felt great. More than that, it felt right. It planted a seed in me, which I can honestly say was the beginning of this book.

Not too long ago, I agreed to give a twenty-minute lecture about health and dance, and it turned into two hours. Again, I felt that high from connecting with the audience, from sharing what I had learned. I began to look at my experiences as life lessons. What could they teach me? What was the purpose of my pain and suffering if not to make me a better, stronger person who is more equipped to lead? You know the old saying "What doesn't kill you makes you stronger." I think it's more than that. I think what doesn't kill you makes you wiser and a better human being. It opens your eyes, your heart, and your mind. You may not have control over everything that happens to you in your life externally, but you always have some control over what's going on internally—how you handle your life experiences and what you take away from them.

In each chapter, I want to share with you the lessons I've learned. And if I make you pause for a moment and consider your own experiences as stepping-stones to taking the lead in your life, then I've done my job. I never imagined myself as a teacher—I was the worst student in school, the one you would vote most likely *not* to succeed. But now, I want to continue to learn more about myself and about human behavior. We all have God-given talent. The question is, what are you going to do with it?

I went to see the musical *Pippin* on Broadway with my Season 10 *DWTS* partner, Nicole Scherzinger. There's this great line in the song "Corner of the Sky": "Don't you see I want my life to be something more than long?" I can relate. I want to leave my footprint on this world in a positive, meaningful way. I want to lead by example. To do that takes a lot of introspection. It also takes courage. I try and see it as connecting the dots—the way I used to try and spot the constellations from my rooftop by drawing imaginary lines between the stars. Every moment in your life should be meaningful; each one should have a takeaway lesson. At the end of every chapter, you'll find mine.

Speak up.

Bullying can be physical, verbal, or emotional—words and threats are just as painful as fists. I know now that the worst thing you can do is suffer in silence. The bullies are counting on you to keep your mouth shut. By doing so, you're giving them even more power. I understand the desire to leave it outside your front door, to just pretend the bullying doesn't happen. In my case, I kept quiet because I was certain that tattling would make my situation worse. Either the brothers would kill me for telling, or my parents would confine me to my house to protect me from all things evil. I was convinced it was a lose-lose situation. But I realize now that I was wrong, and if I could go back and talk to my six-year-old self I would tell him to trust someone and get help—from a parent, an older sibling, a teacher. You're not a wimp if you tell. In fact, seeking help requires incredible strength and courage. The most powerful weapon you have is your voice.

Nowadays, it's easy to bully by hiding behind a phone or a computer screen. The words that people express on Facebook, Instagram, whatever—they're just as cutting and painful as a physical blow. I discovered this when I entered the public eye. Social media has become a playground for cowardly, insecure individuals who unfortunately feel the need to direct negative comments and energy at someone they don't even know. At first I reacted to it. Every obnoxious remark used to dwell in my mind. But the more I learned about human behavior, the clearer it became that the negativity these people project is a reflection of who they are. I don't believe it makes them bad people, but they are seeking a significance that they are not getting elsewhere. Realizing this makes it much easier for me to ignore the haters and not take the bait.

Power over others is weakness in disguise.

People talk a lot about how bullying can destroy your life. For me, it's been a revelation. I got hit in the head a lot of times in my childhood, so maybe it finally knocked some sense into me. I understand now that someone who is strong and loves himself would only ever give love back. The superior human being will always see the light in someone and choose to encourage that light instead of dimming it. Those brothers? They needed to control me because they wanted to feel important. They craved attention and resorted to violence to get it. They needed to control me because they were weak. Looking back now, I actually feel sorry for them. I don't feel like the victim anymore; I was a witness to their suffering. It's helped me move past the pain and fear and make peace with this part of my past. Kids tend to blame themselves when they're bullied—as if something they have done is causing some mean kid to beat the crap out of them. But I see now it was never about me. I did nothing to these brothers. I didn't provoke them; I didn't ask for trouble. They simply saw an easy prey. I ask myself over and over what must have been going on in their heads to make them unleash such wrath on me and my family? What kind of personal pain or insecurity was behind it? Trying to understand helps me let go of the anger and begin to forgive.

Bullies come in all shapes and forms.

Adults can be bullies as well, so be wary of the people around you who try to twist your arm into doing their bidding. You know the type: "My way or the highway." I've met a lot of these manipulators over the years—people who seem nice but are really all about using you or belittling you for their own gain. There are two ways to be the tallest building in a city. You can work hard, build a team, and do the right things to create a huge skyscraper. Or you can tear down all the other buildings around you. That's what bullies do. They think they're big, but it's an illusion. How about coworkers who try and turn the boss against you to make themselves look better? Or someone who's always dumping her dirty work on you because you're kind enough to offer help? Here's the interesting part: these grown-up bullies were most likely bullies as kids or bullied themselves. The same rules apply: Be smart about the situation you're in. Stand up for yourself, say no to their unreasonable demands, and don't allow them to worm their way into your head or your life.

REFLECTING ON DEREK

"Derek thinks of others before he thinks of himself. He's very selfless and motivated by giving joy to other people. He just told me, "I'm so overwhelmed and have so much going on, but that's always the time I do the best work." It's so true. When it's do or die, he's a doer. He's such a great teacher because he wants others to have joy, confidence, and strength. He grew up with all sisters and several female dance partners, and he teaches women to dance on *DWTS*. It's no wonder he's very in tune with how we think and feel. He makes women truly believe in themselves—not just because he's telling them they're beautiful and strong but because he really believes it."

—JULIANNE HOUGH

2

GIRLS AND MORE GIRLS

ONE OF THE dance studio owners had six daughters, and one of them—her name was Autumn "Gypsy" DelGrosso—was my age and looking for a partner for dance competitions. It was kind of a no-brainer, because I had a huge crush on her. She was very religious, and I remember trying really hard to be "spiritual" so she'd like me. Whenever I saw her coming, I'd kneel down and pretend I was praying. I'd quote Scripture in casual conversation, carry a Bible in my dance bag—anything to make her see how "devout" I was. It was a pretty bizarre way to impress a girl, but hey, whatever works!

When I was a little boy, girls were my motivation for most things. I certainly didn't look like a stud—I was a scrawny little runt with white-blond hair and two front teeth missing (I knocked them out leaping off my couch, and it took forever for the adult teeth to grow in). But I had four sisters, and this gave me a great advantage with girls. I thought I understood the female mind. I would eavesdrop on my sisters' conversations about boys and use the information I gleaned to my advantage. I would always tell myself I had the inside track.

I was constantly writing girls love letters or "roses are red" poems professing my undying devotion—a hopeless romantic at seven years old. One day, my second-grade teacher, Mrs. Fox, scolded me for kissing a girl. It was "highly inappropriate" according to her, but I couldn't help it. The girl's name was Elizabeth, and I was smitten.

"Derek, if you want to do something nice for her, bring her a trophy," Mrs. Fox told me.

"A trophy?" I asked. "How is that better than a kiss?"

But I did as she suggested. I went home and got my little plastic soccer trophy that my team had won and handed it to Elizabeth the next day. "I think I'm supposed to give this to you," I told her. She was confused (as was I) but took it, and returned it to me at the end of the day. She must have been somewhat impressed, because I got a kiss back. Not bad. Maybe my teacher did know something.

But no dime-store trophy or love letter was going to win over Autumn DelGrosso. So I volunteered to be her partner. It gave me a purpose beyond getting into trouble. We rehearsed a couple of days a week after school, sometimes into the night, and I didn't complain once. I loved it, even if getting to the studio and home every day was quite a haul. It took my mom forty minutes each way from South Jordan to Orem. On our way, we would pass this landmark called Point of the Mountain, and once, during a bad winter storm, just as we reached it, our car skidded and we got into an accident. It was a very dangerous spot, a place where several people had been killed. We were okay, but every time we drove past the Point during the winter, I held my breath. I thought at any moment we might lose traction in the snow and that would be it. That we continued braving that road was a testament to my dedication to dancing—and to my mom's dedication to getting me there.

In the beginning, I was a rebel at the studio. Most of the students had religion and were so upstanding and moral. I found the pack of boys who were troublemakers and joined them. They taught me a lot: if I didn't have spare change, I could stick my hand up the chutes of the vending machines and steal chips and a can of soda. Fighting was fun— even if it occasionally got too heated. We would roughhouse and wrestle in the dressing room until our coach, Rick Robinson, would come in yelling, "Break it up! What are you trying to do, kill each other?"

We'd start little fires in the grassy area behind the studio (not to burn anything down, just because it was fun) and break into high school campuses at night. It was all in good fun—we weren't thinking about how dangerous it could be. We just liked the thrill of doing something we weren't supposed to do and the rush of potentially being caught.

Autumn was a good girl, and her family saw past my occasional bad behavior and welcomed me. I stayed over a few times at their house and put on quite a show. I used to have night terrors—I would wake up in the middle of the night screaming bloody murder. In the morning, I wouldn't remember any of it. So the first morning, I came to the breakfast table and Autumn looked at me like I had two heads.

"Are you okay?" she asked, gently. I was flattered that she seemed worried about me, but I didn't have a clue what she was talking about.

"Yeah. Why?" She told me I had scared the heck out of the entire family with my screaming. I seemed awake—my eyes were wide open and staring into space—but nothing they could do or say would calm me down. I was in some kind of trance, thrashing around and seeing an imaginary threat that I was helpless to stop. After a few minutes, I settled down and went right back to sleep. Experts say it's like sleepwalking—you're never aware of it—and that it's common in young children, especially ones that are stressed. That didn't make me feel any less mortified in front of Autumn.

I shrugged and tried to make it seem like no big deal. "I'm fine," I insisted, and stuffed my face with pancakes. I knew I had some fears that were surfacing at night through my dreams, but I didn't want anyone—especially Autumn—to know.

At the studio, I could put it all behind me and live in the moment. Because I could master any move they threw at me, I quickly became the teachers' pet. This was a new one for me. I had *never* had a teacher think of me as anything but a goofy good-for-nothing. In the studio, I wanted to excel. If they said, "Jump!" I'd say, "How high—and do you want me to do it backward and blindfolded?" No arguing, no distractions, no veering off in a million different directions. I'd found the solution to my hyperactive mind. I felt focused in a way I'd never been before, as if someone had suddenly changed the radio station and there was no more static. I wanted every dance to be perfect, so if anyone talked or joked around during class, I told them to shut up and pay attention. The older boys didn't appreciate it and called me a kiss-ass, but I wasn't. When I was in class, I was in class. I was there to work and grow. The kids might not have liked me for it at first, but at least they understood where I was coming from. We all had a similar goal.

I wanted to win a dance competition. At this age, it wasn't about the affirmation. It was more about being a member of the studio and the team effort. I wanted to belong. I definitely felt a seed being planted in me. The way the music made me feel, and having the ability to communicate and magnify it through my physicality, was thrilling. If I look back, that's where my passion was born, in those early days at Center Stage.

Though all my sisters danced, I was the only one competing with a partner. It meant more hours in the studio, more training. I counted down the days till our first competition. It was at some random high school in Utah, a small competition to show off what a studio could do. Autumn wore a pink ruffled dress and I was in this horrific skin-tight turtleneck and black trousers. I was so skinny, and I looked like Gumby in that getup. Utah has lots of rules about dance competition costumes—nothing too sexy, nothing too slick—but we had definite flair despite the lame outfits. We owned it.

Most ballroom competitions work the same way. You have about a hundred couples competing, so two hundred people in total. At the beginning of the day you each get a number on your back (from 1 to 100) and based on your number, you dance in a certain heat. Heat 1 goes first, and the type of dance is announced—usually the rhythmic and fast-paced cha-cha to start things off. The cha-cha is a pretty stationary dance, but when you move into samba, it's a traveling dance. You move counterclockwise. You're certain about your partner, but not about your competitors and where they're going to maneuver on the floor. A couple might cut in front of you and you'll have to adjust the routine to go in another direction. Your partnership has to be solid so you can trust each other, communicate, and do this without looking like you've messed up.

After the opening cha-cha, there's usually a long break before the next time you hit the floor, because all the heats have to dance. When you're up again, it's a different style of dance—the samba, followed by the waiting game again. In the course of the day, there are five dances: cha-cha, samba, rumba, paso doble, and jive. If you make the semifinals, you dance all five back to back. The finals are the same, only with fewer bodies. It's relentless; you're going from 9 A.M. till midnight. And you have to dance full out, keep up your stamina, and show that you are skilled and unique enough to be a champion.

Autumn and I might not have been the most technical dancers, but we always tried to be entertaining. I owe that to Coach Rick. He was all about the energy and dancing full-out. "If you want to get down on the floor and do the worm, then do it!" he told me. This was extremely unconventional for a Latin or ballroom competition. He gave me permission to follow my instincts, so I decided we were not going to play by all the rules or follow the status quo. Other studios prided themselves on their technique, but our studio felt like we were "the Performers." If that meant in the middle of my jive I suddenly busted out doing something crazy and unexpected, then so be it.

Inspiration tended to strike when I least expected it. I remem-

ber once during a competition, I saw someone in the audience holding a bouquet of roses. I ran out and grabbed a single stem and put
it between my teeth. Another time, I stole a glass of water out of
someone's hand and took a long sip. Those were the moments when
I started to create an identity for myself as a dancer. If an instinct hit
me, then I just went with it. I might get knocked down for technical
points, but the audience would eat it up. All I could think about was
the next competition . . . and the next . . . and the next.

LEADING LESSONS
March to your own beat.

Dance competitions were always about following the rules—but that
never seemed to hold me back. I didn't always stick to the required
elements or do what everyone else was doing. My teachers were very
encouraging about me putting my own unique spin on things. That
lesson stuck with me. Today, if something is expected of me, I'm going
to challenge it. On *Dancing with the Stars*, I hate being complacent,
which is why I do things that are a little outside of the box. Sometimes
I take a hit for it; sometimes I get a perfect 30. Case in point: the
paso doble I performed with Kellie Pickler and Tristan MacManus
in Season 16. Okay, it was a little avant-garde and edgy; my idea was
to create this parallel universe. Len got a little heated up ("It was a
hodgepodge!"); he thought it was lacking some technical aspects and
gave us a 7, while the other judges gave it a perfect 10. Their disagree-
ment got a lot of press.

So here's the thing: If you go through your life always trying to
please everyone, you're going to let yourself down. You can't rely on
other people to make you feel good. You have to own your choices—
good and bad—because they are yours, and regardless of the outcome, if you choose to, you'll learn from them. One of my challenges

is that I *do* like to please people. But I have to remind myself to be true to who I am, what I feel, and what my instincts are telling me. Often, those instincts are very faint and quiet; you need to listen for them. Even if people don't understand or approve of your choices, in the end, they'll respect you more. I never intend to push the envelope; I intend to push myself. The fear of not improving and growing is greater than the fear of displeasing a judge. It's more important for me to feel I'm progressing and creating new things.

Figure out your passion and everything else will fall into place.

As a kid with raging hormones, I started out thinking that passion meant having the hots for someone. I quickly learned it's much more than that. It's the key to finding your purpose and igniting your soul. Everyone has a passion, whether or not they realize it at this moment. It's there, but sometimes you have to try different vehicles to arrive at something that connects to you. It's almost a magnetic field, pulling you in a direction, not pushing you. It doesn't feel forced or strained in any way. It's natural; it's genuine; it's effortless. One of my greatest mentors, Corky Ballas, showed me that a dance without passion is stiff and awkward; a life without passion is gray and empty. Other people were more technical and skilled dancers than I was, but I learned at a young age that's not what it's all about. It's the fire—the energy, the charisma, the commitment to your emotions—that transforms your performance into something worth watching.

Your passion doesn't have to be a massive goal—not everyone dreams of being a rock star or an Olympic gold medalist. As a kid, I put a lot of pressure on myself to keep winning, but now I see it's more than that. You can find passion in many small ways, on a day-to-day basis. Your passion can be making someone smile or performing an unselfish act. But in each of these small victories, you'll gain momentum in feeling good about yourself, and that's when your ultimate passion—what you're meant to be doing and what truly fulfills you—will reveal itself.

Surround yourself with positive influences.

When I think about the times I've excelled the most in my life, I was always around people who were like-minded and pushed me in a positive way. In order for a plant to grow it needs to be in the right environment and it needs nourishment. My coaches and my fellow students at the studio gave that to me. Likewise, if you put a plant in the dark and you don't ever water it, it's going to die. And if you're not growing, you're dying! So be aware and cautious of your surroundings: Is this the right place for me to grow? You can't choose your family, but you can choose your peers. Love your crazy siblings and parents, but don't hang with people who try to distract you and pull you from your path.

Kids act, adults analyze.

Or I should say we *over*analyze. How many times have you talked yourself out of doing something because it wasn't convenient, practical, profitable, etc.? Recapture that impulsiveness you had as a kid. There was never any psychology behind it; you were simply going with what excited you and living in the moment. No hesitations or apologies. My greatest flaw now is that I think too much, and while I'm busy thinking, an opportunity may pass me by. What happened to that little boy who used to leap before he looked? I'm not saying be reckless, but remember what it was like to act on instinct. Never lose touch with your inner child who understood that some things are definitely worth the risk.

REFLECTING ON DEREK

"Derek and I started dancing together when we were ten years old. I will never forget our first competition. We were competing at BYU in March of 1996. We were offbeat the whole time and ended up placing eighth in the cha-cha. We were so proud of ourselves! After that we improved quickly and it didn't take long for everyone to notice how extremely talented Derek was. We had so much fun dancing together and traveling to many places I never would have gone if it weren't for dance. One of the things that inspired me the most when we were young was the fact that he gave 100 percent every time we danced. Derek was always pushing me to dance the best I could just to keep up with him. I always knew that he was going to accomplish great things in his life. I am so happy for all of his success."

—AUTUMN DELGROSSO

3

STANDING UP

COMPETING STARTED OFF being fun for me, but once I got a taste of winning, a switch flipped in my brain. I didn't want to fall backward; I wanted to win every single time. I started to look at dancing as a sport, and I pushed myself harder and harder: What else could I do that I hadn't tried before? What could I do better? I wouldn't say I was *obsessed* with competing—let's just call it hyperfocused. I wanted to be the best I could be, and nothing else would do. My parents instilled that in my sisters and me.

My mom is a never-take-no-for-an-answer kind of lady. One day, we pulled into a gas station to fix something that wasn't working with the car. The mechanic tinkered with it for about an hour and told us it was fixed. But only a few miles down the road, we realized that wasn't the case. We had to go back; something still wasn't right. My mom tried to explain the problem, but the mechanic was being rude, dismissive, and unhelpful. The guy obviously hated his job and was doing poorly at it. He couldn't have cared less if my mom was unhappy with his work. He took no pride in it whatsoever, and I don't think he had a clue what the words *customer service* are supposed to mean. He made a few more adjustments and sent us on our way. Again, the problem wasn't fixed, so back we went a third time.

As we stood there waiting for him to poke around under the hood some more (and likely do nothing), my mom was getting more frustrated by the moment. Finally, she grabbed my hand and pulled me out of the gas station in a fluster.

"Derek, I don't care what you do," she told me. "You can be a garbageman, a mechanic, a plumber—whatever you want! Just be the best at it." I didn't quite understand what she meant at the time, but those words stuck with me. She wasn't passing judgment on that mechanic—it was a perfectly fine career to have, if he put his heart into it. She just hated to see someone give up, throw in the towel, and not try. My mom could tolerate a lot of things, but a lack of purpose was not one of them.

Purpose was never a problem for me. Dance began to consume my every waking thought—I was going to be the best, and I was impatient for that day to come. I was frustrated that there weren't enough competitions locally to challenge Autumn and me. That's when we started traveling. Attending dance competitions around the country was a huge step toward forging my independence and growing up. When I was younger, I had severe anxiety about sleeping outside of my home. I was such a homebody. A sleepover at my cousin's house turned into a screaming, crying tantrum—I didn't want to be away from my family. But gradually, those fears were overshadowed by the huge excitement of competing. I never stressed about going to some other city if there was a chance of taking home a first-prize trophy.

Autumn and I competed in about a dozen ballroom/Latin competitions—relatively small ones in Idaho and Utah, most of them hosted in school gymnasiums. I also participated in studio competitions where we went as a group from Center Stage. We traveled to

Hawaii, L.A., and New York, and in the midst of the team competitions, I did solo competitions at the L.A. Underground and the New York City Dance Alliance. I won the junior regionals for NYC Dance Alliance in Utah, and I got invited to go to New York to compete at the Waldorf Astoria hotel.

My dad never held me back from going, but he was always afraid for all of his children that we would be let down or rejected. He didn't want us to get our hopes up and be disappointed. Probably for that reason, he didn't shower us with praise. Whatever I did, it was "Okay. You can do better." I didn't understand it at the time, but I see now that he wanted to protect us from being hurt. If he was tough or critical, it wasn't that he was being mean. On some level, he wanted to buffer us from hearing it from someone else. He was trying to build us up. He didn't want us going into the world blindly, thinking we were the best thing since sliced bread. He wanted to remind us that in order to achieve greatness, you have to be better than good—you have to be amazing. He set that standard for himself and for all of us. If you want something, you have to work your butt off for it.

So that's what I did. I trained, I competed, I pushed myself a lot harder than any normal eleven-year-old. This did me no favors when it came to my social life. I knew my peers would see ballroom dancing as a strange hobby for a boy, so I tried to keep it quiet. This only alienated me more from my peers; now I was a loner with a secret life.

Things went from bad to worse. After my parents divorced (that's a whole other story I'll share with you later), we moved to an apartment complex in Orem that was walking distance from the studio. My first day at Orem Junior High, an older kid decided to pick on me. He tapped me on the shoulder, and when I turned around he sucker punched me. My head snapped back and I fell to my knees.

"Come on!" he dared me. "Fight."

I was lying there on the ground, blood gushing out of my nose. What had just happened? I cupped my hands over my face and they filled with blood. At this point, kids were gathering around to watch a fight go down. At that moment, I remembered something my mom told me: "Always fight back. Don't just roll over and take it." So I stood up and threw my blood in his face. It was enough to freak him out momentarily and distract him. Then I jumped on top of him and started pounding him with my fists. Some teachers pulled us apart and dragged me into the principal's office. Even though I hadn't started the fight, even though I was the one with blood pouring out of his nose, I wound up getting expelled from the school. I can't say I was all that sorry. If that's the price I had to pay for standing up for myself, then so be it. Hadn't that been what my mother meant?

When the dust settled, my parents didn't punish me. Most of the time, when I got into trouble with my mom or dad, I could talk my way out of it. I wish I could say that was the last time I got beaten up. A girl in my next junior high either liked me or was trying to make her boyfriend jealous by coming on to me. I was a red-blooded boy with raging hormones, so the attention felt pretty nice. Until her boyfriend and his friends jumped me one day in the track field behind the school. The boyfriend grabbed me around the throat and slammed me facedown on the ground. Two of his friends were holding my arms behind me.

"Dude, if I ever see you around my girl again, I'm going to beat the shit out of you!" Then he kicked me in the stomach, knocking the wind out of me. I tried to be cool about it and walk back with them toward the school. But eventually, I dropped back and ran home. I never looked back or returned to that school, either. I enrolled in another; there were about four in all between elementary and the end of junior high. I couldn't connect to my peers, and I didn't try to. While they worried about their midterm exams or rolling with the popular crowd, all I could think about was bigger and better dance competitions. That was where I belonged.

LEADING LESSONS
Let them see you sweat.

That's what dancing is about. That's what life is about. Basically, you get out what you put in to any situation. If you're lazy, cynical, negative—like that gas station mechanic—it's going to show in anything you do. But if you focus, prepare, give 110 percent, you're a winner no matter what the outcome. Any area of your life that you give attention to—career, relationships, health—will be better. I'm not saying that we should all go out there and become workaholics. I'm saying that you should commit yourself fully; give your whole self to the effort. You can't blame others for your circumstances or your failures. When you ask yourself, "What am I prepared to do?" the answer should always be, "Whatever it takes."

Assert yourself.

When I was in junior high, asserting myself meant standing up to the kid who punched me in the face. As an adult, it means something different. It's not being aggressive, argumentative, or combative. A leader is simply honest about what he or she needs, wants, and feels. This demonstrates self-confidence, self-respect, and dignity. Not being honest shows passiveness, fear, and insecurity. When someone puts you down or walks all over you, don't lie there and act like a doormat. Stand up for yourself. And don't expect people to read your mind. Being assertive requires communication—so it actually improves the quality of your relationships. I admit it: I'm guilty of being a people pleaser sometimes. I hate to disappoint, so I might do or say something that doesn't feel true to me to make someone else happy. It's a tough habit to break, but I'm practicing every day. You can be a nice person without compromising yourself. As a leader, you need to live your life on your own terms without asking people's permission to do so.

Soak up every second of this life that is given to you.

Put your hand on your heart and close your eyes. Maybe you've seen me do this on *DWTS* with my partners backstage before we go on. It calms the nerves and helps you connect to a place of gratitude. You didn't earn your heart; you didn't pay for it. It was given to you as a gift. So take advantage of it, enjoy it, and treat yourself the best way possible. A lot of us are just getting through or managing. Raise your standards. Grow, progress, push yourself, and in turn you will love yourself more. And when you love yourself more, you can love others.

REFLECTING ON DEREK

"Derek is one of the greatest individuals I've ever met, with one of the biggest hearts. When I worked with him, he taught me so much about stepping out of my comfort zone and learning to find confidence in a world that was so foreign. Coming from a professional gymnastics career, I was terrified of letting go and making myself vulnerable in a new art, but every time I did, he would say, "See, I told you you could do it." He's beyond talented, and I often describe him to people as a Mozart. He has a passion and a gift that are unparalleled, and it was a true honor getting to work with him. We started out as strangers, but I will forever be grateful to now call him a true friend."

—SHAWN JOHNSON

4

REAL MEN

W HEN I WAS competing in San Francisco, my dad flew out to
watch me. It was unusual for him; he was usually too busy
with his work to come see me dance. I was happy to spot him in the
audience, but I got a weird feeling in the pit of my stomach: something's wrong. I put it out of my head until the competition was over.
Back in our hotel room, I climbed into bed, ready to collapse from the
whole exhausting day. It was late, after midnight, and the room was
pitch dark. But it was eating away at me, so I had to ask.

"Dad?" I said hesistantly. "Are you and Mom getting a divorce?"

I'm not sure how I knew; I suppose I had sensed the tension
between them for a while. Lately, my dad seemed so deflated. I
couldn't put my finger on what was wrong, but it felt like there was
suddenly a crack in our family foundation. A little kid couldn't see the
reason behind it. Looking back, I have a better grasp on why it happened. My parents, over their more than twenty years together, had
simply drifted apart. It happens in the best of relationships. People's

needs change and the gap between them widens. In my parents' case, distance had a lot to do with it. Besides his work, my dad was the chairman of the Utah Republican Party for two years, and he was gone all the time. I remember only one argument between them, and it wasn't even a big deal. They were simply on two different tracks, and eventually it took its toll.

There was a long silence before my father answered me. "You should ask your mother." That was his way of affirming my suspicions without having to break the painful news. If it weren't true, I told myself, he would have denied it. But I needed to hear it to believe it. It wasn't real until someone said it was.

So right after we got home, I was in the car with my mother and I asked her. It was pouring, and the rain was coming down in sheets on the windshield.

"Mom, are you and Dad getting a divorce?" I asked.

She sighed and took a few minutes to respond. "Yes, probably. But we love you."

And that was it. No further explanation or discussion. The words hung in the air. I tried to wrap my eleven-year-old brain around the truth but couldn't. This wasn't happening—not to us. In the Mormon culture, where family is such a strong unit and marriage is supposed to be eternal, for better and for worse, this made no sense to me.

At the next traffic light, I opened the door and jumped out of the car. My mother called after me but I pretended not to hear her. It was a very dramatic gesture, but drama was my middle name. It was the only way I knew how to express the emotions swirling around inside me. I just kept walking in the rain, unsure of where I was going but convinced I needed to run away. I was confused, sad, angry—a whole bunch of different feelings, none of them good. My mom let me cool off for a few minutes. Then she pulled up next to me and opened the car door, and I got back inside. I was soaked to the bone and made a huge puddle on the seat.

I don't think I said a word the whole rest of the ride, and neither did she. In the following months, there was a separation period and a tense time when my parents tried to work out the details of the divorce. After my initial protest, a calmness came over me. I just wanted them both to be happy. I knew they couldn't find happiness together anymore, and I thought it would be selfish of me to wish that they stayed together under those circumstances. My sisters were less forgiving and philosophical; they were very vocal about how upset they were. I tried to stay neutral, but it was hard. Up until this point, I had always been a mama's boy. But gradually, it became my dad whom I empathized with and saw in a different light.

One day I was home, hanging out in my bedroom downstairs in the basement. My parents' room was directly above mine, and I heard a strange, whimpering sound coming from it. I strained to make it out, then realized it was someone crying. My father.

I didn't know what to do. I had never heard or seen my dad in tears. I could hear him now through the wall, a muffled cry, and it broke my heart. I had always thought of my father as indestructible, bulletproof. Superman had nothing on him. Yet now, he seemed so broken and fragile. Lying there in the dark, listening to him cry, terrified me. It was as if I had lost my concrete. But at the same time, I felt completely helpless; I wanted to run upstairs and throw my arms around him, but I knew it would embarrass him. My dad was always such a proud guy—strong and consistent in his beliefs, the backbone of our family. He would never have wanted me to see him in that condition.

Not that it would make me think any less of him. In fact, it had the opposite effect. From that day on, he seemed more real to me, more human. And when the time came to sell our house and move to an apartment complex in Orem, I chose to live with him over my mother. True, their apartments were adjacent, so I didn't have far to go to visit my mom and sisters, but I felt a stronger connection to my dad. From the time he came to my competition in San Francisco, I had felt a shift in our relationship. He was more present, more thoughtful in small ways. I had always respected him, but I put him high on a pedestal. Now, he felt closer to earth, closer to me.

Of course, I gave him a terrible time at first. We all reacted to the divorce in different ways. My three older sisters were almost all grown up—Sharee was about to be married—so they needed our parents less in their day-to-day lives. Julianne was little, so I'm not sure how much she understood. I got it; I knew what it meant. I knew how people would talk around the neighborhood and in church, how they would look down on us with pity and disapproval. I would be one of "those" kids—the ones that came from a broken home. I decided I might as well live up to the role, so I began to cut school and skip dance class and hang around with a bad crowd. If my mom or dad scolded me, or a dance coach asked why I had missed rehearsal, I gave them all attitude. Wasn't that what kids from broken homes did? Wasn't it now my job to be a wise-ass screw-up? It became my new identity for several months until a couple of people finally talked some sense into me and reminded me who I really was.

Those amazing people were Corky and Shirley Ballas.

LEADING LESSONS
You become the person you think you are.

In a matter of weeks after my parents announced their divorce, I underwent a total personality transformation. I was like Dr. Jekyll and Mr. Hyde: a new Derek took over. I assumed I was bad news—the boy from the broken family—so that is who I became. I see now that this was my coping mechanism; the only way I could deal with the pain and loss was to become someone else, someone tougher who didn't care about anything. It was denial and it was lashing out. I knew my parents would be upset and disappointed if I got into trouble. On some level, it was payback. But what I see now is an important lesson: our thoughts have great power. If I believe I am strong, smart, capable, then I become those qualities. Sometimes you find yourself in the center of a raging storm. Will you run away, duck for cover, or stand tall and weather it? The divorce was the end of the world as I knew it, and I assumed I was collateral damage. But who was I hurting? My parents or myself?

I like to remind myself of this story: A man with two sons commits a crime and goes to jail for life. One son grows up to be successful and happy with a wife and family; the other ends up a criminal and in jail. When an interviewer asks each one how they wound up where they are, they have the same reply: "How could I NOT be where I am with a father like mine?" Same experience, same father, but each son found a different meaning and purpose in what they went through.

I won't say the divorce was easy on any of us. But now I look back on it as the beginning of my growing up and making the right choices. Because of it, I eventually threw myself into dance and traveled all around the world. Had the divorce not happened, had I not been so troubled by it, I'm not sure I would have ever recognized my opportunity to succeed.

Fast-forward fifteen years, and I wouldn't have things any other way. The divorce was the moment that defined my entire family, as a whole and as individuals. My mom is more independent and strong because of the divorce, and my dad is a better man because of it—more compassionate and loving. So much good has come from it. I also understand it so much better. As human beings, no matter where we're from or what color we are, we're all struggling with the same needs. We all want to feel connected—to God, to our work, to our parents, to our loved ones. We need to meet those needs. In my parents' marriage, that was no longer happening, so my mom had to move on. I see now it was not just her right, but her obligation to herself. And I would never hold that against anyone.

There's no point in pointing a finger.

Blame is useless. At first, yes, I did a hold a grudge against my mother. At the time, in my mind, she broke up the Hough family; she set the wheels in motion by leaving my father. I was hurt and I was angry and I needed to dump that all somewhere. But if I'm going to blame her for splintering the family, then I also have to give her credit for the good that came from it. Because of the divorce, I am a more compassionate person. Because of it, I learned how to love more deeply. Because of it, I grew into the man I am today. My mom is the most caring, loving, amazing woman on the planet. Nobody has a bigger heart than she does. So the blame was misplaced; it often is. We blame others when we feel control slipping through our fingertips, or when we think we are in the wrong and it feels better to pin it on someone else. In my case, the rug was pulled out from under me and I was struggling to make sense of it. Mom was an easy target. But leaders don't shirk responsibility. They accept it, even if they're not at fault, because they know how much can be learned in the process. We're all human; we all make mistakes. What if instead of assigning the blame for something that went wrong, you accept the responsibility for what you can do to make it right?

Vulnerability does not take away your strength.

Hearing my father cry was scary at first—he was "the Man." But it also made me see that someone who was a strong leader could still feel and express feelings of hurt. It gave me permission to be vulnerable in my life. It allowed me to open up, and in some ways, it changed my definition of masculinity. You don't have to be stoic; you don't have to always take it on the chin. A real man is never afraid to express what's in his heart and soul. In my mind, that's the definition of strength, and I learned it from my father.

REFLECTING ON DEREK

"Being present for Derek's creative process is a true privilege. To see his energy and enthusiasm surrounding each idea is something very special. I found Derek's excitement toward creating movement to be absolutely infectious."

—MERYL DAVIS

5

YOU WIN SOME, YOU LOSE SOME

B LACKPOOL DANCE FESTIVAL in England is the Super Bowl of ballroom dancing. It's been going on for eighty years, and to compete there—even in the junior preteen division—you have to be at the top of your game. Rick decided Autumn and I were ready for it. It was the first time I would be traveling out of the country—five thousand miles from home. I couldn't wait to get on that plane. My mom would tell me stories about some of her family in Idaho who never left their hometown, and I assured her that would never be me. The idea of traveling was one of my biggest motivators for staying with dance—pretty funny for a kid who had been afraid to sleep away from his own bed for so many years. My dad came over with us; he was an experienced traveler, and he wanted to be there for my first time out of the country.

Our first stop was London, where there were a few competitions leading up to Blackpool. I had never seen this level of competition before. I was so excited by the energy and the feeling of being around all these amazing dancers. I wasn't overwhelmed, just a little embarrassed. Everyone looked so polished, and they all smelled like fancy cologne. Comparatively, I looked and felt like the poor kid on the block. I didn't own the proper costume (white tie, black jacket, and black trousers), so I'd rented one from a wedding store before we left home. It was baggy in all the wrong places, and I didn't have the right shoes.

Watching the dancers get ready backstage, we realized we were also completely unprepared. They'd put water or castor oil on the floor and rub the soles of their shoes in it. Then they'd scratch the soles with a wire brush, roughening up the suede to prevent slipping. As we stepped out for the first round, Autumn spit in the middle of the dance floor and rubbed her feet in it. She encouraged me to do the same, so I did—hoping that not too many people were watching. I remember thinking, Yeah, we are *definitely* from out of town.

When we got to Blackpool, it was even more posh than the London competitions. The Blackpool Tower Ballroom is enormous and dates back to 1894—so it was like stepping back in time. There is a mile-high vaulted ceiling, walls decorated with murals, and two tiers of balconies for the audience to sit and watch. The dance floor is made up of thirty thousand blocks of mahogany, oak, and walnut assembled in an intricate pattern.

I had never seen anything like it. There were thousands of people from all over the globe dancing, and I could feel the adrenaline kick in. I was meant to be here. I was meant to be in this world. I closed my eyes and pictured myself accepting the trophy as the crowd went wild. But our competitors were fierce: their moves were razor sharp, and we struggled to keep up. We did all the dances, then there was a break where we waited for our number to be called. It wasn't, and that was it. We were knocked out in the first round.

I was in shock: everyone was so good and we were out of their league. At Center Stage, I was the big man on campus. Here? A has-been by round 1. It took me down a notch and made me think hard and long about why I wasn't living up to my potential. I knew I had it in me, but I also knew I had a lot more work to do. I knew training in a studio in Orem was probably not going to get me to that level. Looking around the ballroom, I saw my future. All I had to do was fight for it and make it happen.

But I can't say the trip was a total wash—while I was in England, I met a girl (big surprise!). Her name was Jade Main, and she was a pretty little blonde with blue eyes from Birmingham, England. In between rounds, we hung out on the jungle gym in the building. I chased her around and when I caught her, I leaned in and gave her a kiss. I swear, violins started playing in my head! I was always this little kid with a huge imagination, trying to live in a movie. I had just seen *Titanic*, so I romanticized the entire encounter. I pictured myself in the role of the scruffy American boy; Jade was the noble British girl. And of course, in my mind, ours would be the love of a lifetime.

Because I convinced myself of this, I couldn't bear the thought of leaving her. My dad was anxious to go to Scotland the next day and show me the sights. I bawled for the entire drive there.

"She's the love of my life!" I said.

"Derek," my father sighed. "You're eleven years old. Trust me. You're going to meet a lot of other girls."

"You don't understand!" I sobbed. "She's the one."

He took me to Edinburgh Castle and even gave me my first taste of haggis (a pudding made with a sheep's heart, lungs, and liver). I didn't even find that cool; I was beside myself and being so melodramatic. Looking back on it, I can't tell you why I felt so strongly. I was a kid; I was in another country; she was a cute girl. All my emotions got tangled up and blown out of proportion.

On the flight home, I wrote Jade a seven-page note and dotted it with water droplets to look like tears. Hilarious. Of course I never mailed it, but I fantasized that Jade would be waiting and we'd meet again someday. Shortly after we got home, my dad dropped me off at scout camp at Fish Lake, where I worked on my merit badges. While I was learning how to tie knots and make my own shelter out of twigs and twine, I once again thought of my lost love. I made her a necklace out of a jade stone and some leather cord, and vowed I'd give it to her when we were reunited.

The next day, I found out there was a Girl Scout camp not far from ours. It was just the distraction I needed to gain my sanity back. I met this girl, and I swear to you, I have no recollection what she looked like or what her name was. I just remember feeling super excited that I was about to go into a tent and make out with her. She was sixteen—a way older woman—and for some reason, she was into it. So I buried my broken heart and moved on. Funny how that happens.

My first trip to London was an eye-opener. It put me in an environment where everyone was better than me. As humbling as that was, it was also a tremendous motivation. I knew I would have a lot of work to do before I went back. I needed to raise my standards to be able to compete with the best—and eventually, one day, to beat them. The amazing thing was that I never doubted it would happen. I wasn't being cocky or conceited; I just knew what I could do if I put my mind to it.

LEADING LESSONS
It's the failures that make us winners.

When you win a competition, you celebrate. You are on cloud nine. But when you lose, you learn. In my case, losing Blackpool that first time was the best thing that ever happened to me. I dug deep down and asked myself what it was that was holding me back from achieving what I knew I was capable of. Failure shows you what's possible.

It makes your desire burn hotter. It builds courage, and in the end, it makes the win that much sweeter. I would rather fail at something than regret never trying. Leaders think of failures as experiments, showing them what works and what doesn't and how to fix things. We live in a world where failure is thought of as something negative: no one likes the idea of screwing up. But what if you could change that? What if you could see failure as a positive? What if you could embrace failure as part of the process necessary to get what you want? Suddenly, the fear of it disappears. I never went into any competition wanting to fail (just the opposite), but after racking up my share of disappointments, I learned that I could deal with it. It hurt and pissed me off at the time, but now I see the value in it. I wouldn't be where I am today without those failures notched on my belt.

Never be the best in the room.

The champions in life—in every field of endeavor—feel the constant challenge to take the content up a notch. Champions know that if we are not stretching and pushing ourselves to our ultimate capacity and potential as human beings, someone else, somewhere else, is.

A little girl came up to me recently and asked if I had any advice for her on how to be a better dancer. She acted very grown-up for a seven-year-old. She really wanted me to give her some good, concrete tips. So she pulled up a chair at my table, rested her chin in her hands, and stared at me. Talk about pressure! In that moment, I tried to find something more constructive to tell her than just, "Practice hard." I thought to myself, what was it that helped me improve?

"Are you the best in your class?" I asked her.

"Yes," she replied.

"Then you have to go into a class where there are people who are better than you."

She raised an eyebrow. "Why?"

"Because being around older, more experienced dancers is what pushed me to become better. You need the challenge."

The kid nodded. It made sense (phew!). People always ask me if I was inspired by Gene Kelly or Fred Astaire. Truth be told, I never saw their movies when I was young. The people I emulated were the ones I practiced with and competed against. Going to Blackpool made me see the level that I needed to be at and the people I needed to be around in order for me to take it to that level.

6

MY SECOND PARENTS

O NE DAY, AN odd couple strolled into Center Stage Studio. Their names were Corky and Shirley Ballas, and they definitely stood out. Shirley was very "put together": hair done up, designer clothing from head to toe, gold jewelry dripping. Corky's heritage was part Spanish, part Greek, and he had jet-black hair, very strong, prominent features, and slightly wild eyes.

"Are they dancers?" I naively asked one of the older students in my class.

"Dancers? They're world champions! They're legends!"

He wasn't kidding. In the nineties, the Ballases were known as the best of the best in ballroom. Shirley had been a world champ at nineteen with her ex-husband. When Corky came into her life, he was a ballroom beginner. He was from Texas, and his dad, George Ballas, was the inventor of the Weed Eater. It took Corky and Shirley ten years to become champions, but they didn't rest until they had the title. All the teachers and the studio owners were in awe of them.

Once you won a world championship, you usually toured the world teaching and visiting various studios. The Ballases had been going to Provo, Utah, to train the Brigham Young University Latin team since the early nineties, and while visiting, they were approached by Center Stage to teach at the studio for several weeks at a time.

I was skeptical at first, especially because Corky seemed like such a wild card. He was outgoing, silly, and (as his name seemed to imply) very quirky. He delivered his Latin dance class like a Chris Rock stand-up routine, going off on long rants and emphasizing his words with dramatic body movement. When he spoke it was very theatrical. But after just one day, I realized how amazing these two were, both individually and together. They balanced each other perfectly: energy meets elegance, passion meets precision. And they were a whole other level of dancer, with an expertise I had never witnessed before.

So I wiggled my way into the front row of every one of their classes. Corky was hilarious and the coolest guy ever. Shirley was kind of a hard-ass. I say that with the utmost love and admiration, and I know she wears that title with pride. The woman was all about technique, and she never sugarcoated anything. If you screwed up, she told you so: "Derek, that was awful."

Or she would make you do it over, and over, and over—a dozen or more times if necessary—till she was satisfied. Sometimes my head would pound and my legs would ache, but she kept pushing me and taunting me: "No, not like that. That's rubbish!" There was just no filter on her—what was in her head came out of her mouth. When we first met, I was a kid with only about six months' dance experience under my belt, and she scared me a little. Still, I really wanted to make her happy. So I worked harder than I ever had before, just trying to coax a single word out of Shirley: "Good."

Corky, as I said, was different: a fireball of energy and a real jokester. I was the youngest in Corky's class and I think he got a kick out of me—the short little blond boy trying to best all the adults in his class. One day, I came into Studio 5 and there were these plastic baseball bats on the floor. No one was around, so Corky started hitting one baseball bat on the ground with a single-time beat. I grabbed two other bats and started doing syncopated times and layering more beats over that. We were just sitting there, smiling and laughing, creating something really cool out of nothing. No drum set, no sticks, just picking up whatever was lying around and setting it into motion. I loved it. I felt inspired. Here was someone who not only shared my creativity but could teach me even more.

The Ballases will tell you that they remember me back then as "the little blue-eyed boy with shiny penny loafers." They saw in me a restlessness, a burning for knowledge. I was quick on my feet, though not the most technically proficient dancer in the studio. What I needed was direction, guidance, clarity.

I felt so excited every day to come in to learn from them—and I wanted to make that perfectly clear. So on the second day of class, I waited at their car and presented them with a drawing I had done and signed with a flourish. Shirley hung it on the studio wall. The next day, I came with a shiny apple. Some of their classes were age restricted, but they allowed me to attend all of them. It didn't matter; I could outdance 95 percent of the teenagers and young adults there. The studio was the only place I wanted to be. I even slept there as I grappled with the news of my parents' divorce. When I was going through my darker days—skipping school, blowing off dance class—it was Corky and Shirley who noticed and asked where I'd been. They had gone away for six weeks to perform out of state, and when they returned, there was no one waiting at their car with a gift or greeting.

The other teachers told them I had been missing classes, cutting school, and getting into all sorts of mischief. Shirley knew it would take a hell of a lot to keep me away from her classes, and she was worried. When she heard what was happening in my home life, she understood and knew she had to intervene. I was lost, and heading down a slippery slope. There seemed only one solution: "Come live with us in England, study dance, compete, and see the world." I wanted to rush home at that moment and pack my bags. I saw it as a once-in-a-lifetime golden opportunity. How many eleven-year-olds from Utah get to go live in England and travel the world? I didn't even have to think about it. I was ready to leave right then and there. But we still had to convince my parents. I don't know how excited they were for me to live so far away from home, but Shirley told them it would be for the best. "He's got promise," she said. "And he'll be a good companion for our son, Mark."

Had my parents still been married, I'm sure the answer would have been no. But since everything at home was so unstable, this seemed a good temporary solution. Clearly, I was not dealing well with the divorce and needed something to take my mind off it. They agreed it would be a good thing for me to get away until the dust settled.

So I recommitted myself to my dancing. I swore up and down to Shirley that there would be no more shenanigans. I'd buckle down, stop acting like a brat, and get over myself. Shirley expected me to play by her rules. Of course, that was all before I got to know her son, Mark Ballas, and we became partners in crime.

Mark is now one of my *DWTS* compadres and one of my best friends. I consider him a brother. We've known each other for fifteen years and we've been on eleven seasons together. But when we first met, we hated each other. Total oil and water. I thought he was a stuck-up, royal pain in the ass. We were in Studio 2 at Center Stage, which had a ballet room you are not supposed to even walk into wearing tennis sneakers. Apparently, Mark never got the memo. He just zipped right in there on his K2 Fatty inline skates. He was the spitting image of his dad, a mini Corky, and a year younger than I was—about ten at the time. But he had such a sense of entitlement!

"You can't wear those blades in here," I told him.

He smirked and continued scuffing up the floor, as if no one could touch him.

"Hey!" I yelled. "Get out of here with those!"

Again, it was as if I were talking to a brick wall. Given who his parents were, I thought it best not to take it any further—although I would have loved to have mopped the floor up with him!

Mark and I were different. He was really into rock and heavy metal music—bands like Nirvana and Korn.

"You know that that's the devil's music, right?" I asked him. I guess some of my Mormon upbringing had stuck. I even got Shirley to snap one of his Green Day CDs in half.

He thought I was an idiot. We were opposite in so many ways. When we first started hanging out, he came back to my place and I showed him my drums. It was the first time he had played an instrument, and he got really into it, banging away. I had this smelly fart spray in my pocket and thought it would be a really funny joke if I sprayed it near him. He thought I sprayed it *on* him and freaked. He was hopping mad and started beating me over the head with the drumsticks.

I really thought he was the biggest spoiled brat, yet there was something about him that I liked. Maybe it was the fact that he was always able to speak to his parents so openly, almost as if he were their equal, even at a young age. Sometimes I was shocked to hear some of the things that came out of his mouth, but I was always in awe of his honesty.

When we first arrived in London, I was so naive. "Wait! They all drive cars here?" I asked Mark. He just rolled his eyes and dragged me along by the elbow. I wasn't sure what to expect of my new digs in Dulwich Village, a nice neighborhood in South London. I had only been to England once before—the time we competed at Blackpool— and I had barely set foot outside of the ballroom or the airport. I had a pretty romanticized vision of what it would be like. I thought people would be driving around in horse-drawn carriages, wearing monocles and morning coats, and sipping tea all day. Instead it was just a busy city, filled with hustle and bustle and modern conveniences. Mark wanted to know what planet I was from.

He was born in Texas, but had been living in London for several years. This was his home. Shirley and Corky had consulted him before asking me to live with them. They wanted to be perfectly clear: Mark would need to learn to share *everything*, including his room and his toys, and there would be no kicking me out if we had a fight. It was his decision as much as theirs to invite me in.

As curious as I was about London, people were curious about me. I got a lot of funny looks: "Who is this strange American kid moving in with Corky and Shirley Ballas?" They had never taken in a boarder before; people weren't sure what to make of it. Their house was old but beautiful. I remember the wood-paneled ceiling in the Asian-themed room, the marble fireplace in the living room, and the elaborate chandelier in the dining room. It was all very posh compared to what I was used to in Utah. We had a large backyard and a beautiful park across the street. But the best part? I had never had a brother before, and now I got to experience what that was like.

When we first arrived, Shirley arranged for three different girls to try out to be my dance partner. One of them was Jade. Yes, *that* Jade. I was so happy, and I played out the whole romantic storyline once again in my mind. But when she came into the studio, it was all business. Shirley had me dance with each girl and we evaluated the choices. In the end, I actually didn't want to partner with Jade. I preferred another girl, Leanne Noble, and am not sure Jade ever forgave me for that. It was the end of our romance: the dancing won out over first love.

Besides dance, there was school. Shirley enrolled us in the Italia Conti Academy of Theatre Arts—a co-ed school for kids ages ten and up who were interested in pursuing careers in the arts. It was very prestigious, kind of like the school in *Fame* but in London. To get there, we had to take three trains, and God help us if we were late (Shirley wouldn't stand for it). Every morning, Mark and I would get up at seven and race to make the seven forty-five at Herne Hill station. The Thameslink line was always mobbed, and we'd be packed in like sardines, smelling everyone's underarm deodorant or lack thereof. We rode over the River Thames, past St. Paul's and the London Eye. The huge Ferris wheel wasn't even there when I first moved to London; I actually got to see it being built. The train ride was where I daydreamed and did most of my "deep thinking." I plugged in my minidisc player, listened to my tunes, and stared out the window at the city of London. Then we changed trains to go on the Underground to Barbican. When we got off, we had to walk half a mile to the school. Even in the cold, damp, blustery winter months, I didn't mind. There was a little breakfast place across from the school, and they made toasted bagels with sausage and brown sauce. I actually looked forward to going to school every day just to get my sausage bagel.

School was from 9 A.M. to 6 P.M. In the wintertime, it would be dark when we arrived and dark when we left—we literally never saw sunlight. Italia Conti was the name of the actress who founded the school in 1911. The huge campus is divided into several buildings. Ours was nine stories tall, and we weren't allowed to use the elevators, so we were climbing up and down stairs all day. We wore uniforms— blue blazers, gray slacks, light blue shirts, and blue ties with the logo of the school stitched in white. The teachers there were a cast of colorful characters. My headmaster, Mr. Vote, was this Australian guy. He had a gray beard and hair, and he also taught history. Miss Day, my science teacher, was a large woman who wore half her head shaved and the other half of her hair in a bob. Miss Matkins, my English teacher, was about four foot five and had this squeaky, high-pitched voice. She walked around in high heels with bent legs. When I had to go away to a dance competition, she was kind enough to do my homework for me by telling me all the answers. Mr. Duwitt taught me math. He was an older man, and when he leaned over to show me how to work an equation, the smell of smoke and tobacco on his body was so pungent, it made me gag. His famous expression was "The mind boggles," as in, "Derek, you can learn a complicated dance routine yet not figure out a simple simultaneous equation. The mind boggles!"

Principal Anne Sheward had her office on the ninth floor—so most kids rarely went up there. I, however, was a frequent visitor. I hated ballet class, so I would skip it, and my teacher would angrily march me up the stairs for disciplinary action. But Ms. Sheward was great. She would tell me to take a seat, and we would have a cool chat about life for a few minutes. She never scolded or punished me (though we didn't let my ballet teacher know that). It was a free-spirited school, for sure, and for the first time in my life, I had lots of friends. There was George Maguire, the cool kid and a very talented actor and singer, and Newton Faulkner (then known as Sam), with his ginger hair done in dreadlocks. Sam would skip class and lock himself in the boys' changing room so he could practice chords on his guitar. Fast-forward six or seven years later, and he was signed to a major record label. I always knew he would make it. Lucas Rush and Desi Miller were my two best friends, the ones I got into trouble with the most. They would bust on me every time I tried to talk in a British accent. But teasing aside, I felt encouraged, supported, inspired. The academy was all about letting us be creative and follow our dreams.

During lunch or in between classes, I would go to the art room—I even had my own key. Once again, I became a bit of a loner, but this time by choice. My friends were always asking, "Where's Derek?" and that's where I was hiding. The art room was my sanctuary. My art teacher, Miss Todd, was very eccentric. Her hair was wild, and she dressed like a hipster. She showed me art books filled with paintings and sculptures of naked women. She would take our classes on field trips to all these crazy installations at the Barbican Art Centre and the Tate Modern. Her classes lit my imagination on fire. I didn't have to obsess over straight lines or shading or capturing an image of something down to the exact detail. Until I met her, I had never seen modern art before. She showed me that art doesn't need to be technically perfect; it just needs to mean something. I'd look at some scribbles on a canvas and say, "I can do that." Miss Todd would shake her head and break it down for me. "It's not scribbles. There's a story and an emotion behind it."

After school, I'd take the train home and we'd have dinner. Shirley's mom, Audrey (we called her Nanny), lived with us and made us dinner (spaghetti Bolognese and roast chicken and potatoes were my favorites). Then we'd drive to the Semly Practice Hall, where I ran my dances with my partners from nine to nearly midnight. It was in this terrible neighborhood called Norbury, and to reach the studio I had to climb two flights of creaky stairs. The whole place smelled moldy, sweaty, and damp, and the lights flickered. There was a little stage; Shirley sat and watched me practice. She gave us pointers here and there, but it wasn't about corrections. It was a chance to show off and eye up the competition. Some of the world's greatest dancers practiced there every day.

On a rare night off, Mark got me to go to a Korn concert at Wembley Arena with him. I put my foot in Mark's hand during "Freak on a Leash" and he hoisted me up. I crowd-surfed from the back of Wembley to the front, allowing hundreds of strangers to carry me in their arms. I felt like I was baptized into rock and roll! From there on in, I was hooked on heavy metal music. Shortly after, Mark and I ended up starting a band together—we called it Almost Amy. I drew a cool logo with two A's in it.

"Say the first A word that comes to mind," I told Mark.

I said "Almost" and he said, "Amy." So there we had it!

We eventually turned the beautiful dining room into our jam space. We took out the marble tables, drapes, and chandelier and painted the walls black and the ceiling red. Shirley and Corky let us do it—it was our cave of creation. I played drums and Mark was on electric guitar (my dad bought it for him for Christmas). We wore black eyeliner and nail polish and punked it out. We even got bookings at battles of the bands in local pubs and at the Gilford Rugby Club. It was pretty funny, because our alter egos were competitive Latin dancers—all low-cut shirts and rhinestones. We could slip easily in and out of both personas—whatever the occasion called for.

We lived in a safe, family-friendly area, but parts of London were rough, as you'd expect from any large city. Mark had a knack for attracting muggers. One time, we were in a train station and a little kid—no more than about eight years old—came up to him: "Oi, mate, give me your phone." We always carried the cool Nokia phones with the Snake game on them, and they were the hot item. It was like inviting trouble carrying one around, but we didn't care.

Mark thought the mini-mugger was crazy: "Are you kidding me? No way." Then he looked over his shoulder and realized the kid wasn't alone; he had a whole gang with him. So Mark handed over his phone and the kid ran off. I never let him live down the fact that an eight-year-old had mugged him.

I had my own incident as well, but I handled it a little differently. I got off the train at Herne Hill station and noticed that two guys were following me. I could hear their footsteps getting closer and closer. "Give us your backpack," they threatened me.

"Why? All I have is my homework in here," I tried to reason with them. They had seen me on the train with my minidisc player and they knew I was holding out on them. "Give it," they threatened.

My bag was covered with key chains and buttons, and as I took it off my shoulder, pretending to give it to them, I swung it hard in their faces. All that hardware knocked one of them to the ground and stunned the other. With my bag in hand, I ran the mile home without ever looking back. Not bad for a skinny kid in a school uniform.

I was proud of the person I was becoming in London. I thought I would miss home, but truthfully I didn't. Part of the reason was that there was no time. My days and nights were so jam-packed, I simply functioned on autopilot, going from school to practice and catching a few hours of sleep in between. The other thing that kept me from being homesick was that I knew I was on the right path. I was surrounded by people who believed in me and were taking care of me. So no, I wasn't homesick. In fact, just like the time I ran from those muggers, I never looked back.

LEADING LESSONS
Pounce on an opportunity—even if you think you're not ready.

Whenever I got a new partner—and I had several over the years—I'd want to rehearse for months before we competed. But Shirley would give us two weeks to get five routines down. She'd throw us out there: "You have to bite the bullet." Ready or not, we hit the dance floor. Why? Because you're never ready till you're doing it. No amount of preparation in the world can prepare you for the actual experience. I tell my *Dancing with the Stars* partners this all the time. You can rehearse for weeks, months, years, and still never be *ready*. You have to just go out there and live it—that's when it will all make sense and come together. You can't prepare yourself for the actual in-the-moment experience.

Leaders take that leap. You can't let insecurity hold you back. The walls that protect you are also the walls that imprison you. There's an old Cherokee story about a grandfather who tells his grandson about the two wolves that live inside us all. There's a battle raging between them. One is evil—he represents fear, doubt, self-pity, regret. The other is good—he stands for joy, peace, confidence, truth, faith. The grandson asks, "Which wolf wins?" The old Cherokee simply replies: "The one you feed."

There may never be a right time or a right place to take a risk. The right time is right now. In the past, I used to overanalyze everything, and if something landed in my lap, some great chance to be taken, I'd often talk myself out of it. I know now that you have to have confidence in who you are and what you want. You have to seize the opportunity and feed the good wolf.

Failure can't live in the company of perseverance.

Failure eventually surrenders. Corky and Shirley taught me this. It took them ten years to win Blackpool. Ten years! Some people would give up and throw in the towel after ten minutes! Every time they lost, all the people around them blamed Corky. But he was relentless. He was going to prove his talent not just to the naysayers but also to himself. There were many times as a competitive dancer when I felt deflated and not good enough, but I never gave up—the Ballases never let me. You always have to keep on moving forward and having faith. Think of the greatest leaders we know. What do they all have in common? They all fought some uphill battle to get where they are. Call it tenacity, persistence, or plain old stubbornness. When someone or something tries to push me off my path, that's when I dig my heels in even harder. I'll be honest: in some areas of my life, I have this mastered. In others, I need a little reminder now and then. There's nothing you can't do if you see it through.

Don't jump to conclusions over first impressions.

They're often dead wrong. When I first met Mark, I thought he was spoiled. When I met Shirley, I assumed she was tough as nails. But getting to know them both as a member of their family, I saw how wrong I was. Shirley is a teddy bear, a caring, loving person who would do anything for me. And Mark? I think of him as a brother, in every sense of the word. I've learned to make a special effort to get to know the people who put up walls and seem cold or tough. It's like an onion; you have to peel back the layers. I'm sure some of my *DWTS* partners made an assumption about who I was the first time they worked with me. They probably thought I was a tough task-master and cursed me out for putting them through this! But anyone who truly knows me will tell you, I'm harder on myself than I am on anyone else. And I'm a softie who loves to goof around. But to see that side of me, you need to move past the first impression. What's the lesson here? Dig a little deeper. Get to know people and what makes them tick. Don't make an assumption till you know someone a lot better. Think of all the people you might have dismissed who could have been great friends, mentors, or allies, if you'd only given them the chance.

Perfect example: dancing with Lil' Kim on *DWTS*. She had recently spent time in jail and I remember thinking, Oh my gosh, I'm afraid I'm going to get shanked in the middle of the dance! Then I realized I was judging her without knowing her, something that I have hated people doing to me in the past. It took only a few minutes to see the sweet, loving person she truly was. Had I not given us the chance to get to know each other better, I never would have learned that.

REFLECTING ON DEREK

"Derek's gratitude is endless. He wants the best for himself but truly understands he has to work for it, and work he does. I could not imagine my life without Derek in it—it would be a boring place! He gives back to me in so many ways: kindness, graciousness, caring, love, honesty. He's a great man and teacher, and even though I did not give birth to him, I truly feel he is my son."

—SHIRLEY BALLAS

7

THE BALLAS BRAT PACK

IT WAS THREE months before I went back home to Utah. That was the original plan: I would go abroad, have this great experience, then go home to Orem and get back to my life. That's what my mom and dad had agreed to, and that's what I had promised them.

But in those three months abroad, so much happened. I grew up a lot. I developed a strong focus, discipline, and a desire to compete on a much higher level. That overrode everything else. There was no going back to the way things had been—I'd moved past all of that. I had forged a new identity for myself, and I was a part of a new family. It amazed me how quickly it all fell into place. London felt normal; Utah felt strange.

The dust was settling from the divorce, and my dad especially wanted some semblance of normalcy back. He wanted to be a dad to me, and that was impossible to do with five thousand miles separating us. I pleaded with him to send me back.

"Please," I begged, "I have to go back to London. I'm doing so well there." I could feel myself moving in a forward trajectory, and I was afraid if I came back to Utah, I'd stop progressing. I was ready to work and ready to achieve all the goals that had been set in front of me. In my mind, there was no other option.

While my parents were mulling it over, a problem cropped up with Mark's dance partner. The girl outgrew him—literally. All of a sudden, she was a head taller! So he needed someone new, and fast.

"Hey, maybe you should dance with my sister Julianne!" I teased him. She was all of nine years old at the time, still studying at Center Stage. I could see the wheels turning in Shirley's head as soon as the words came out of my mouth. Julianne was very talented, and she had a maturity to her dancing that was way beyond her years. She had done some competing before, even moved to Florida for a few weeks to work as a couple with a Russian kid.

So Shirley arranged for a little tryout in Studio 6 at Center Stage. Mark and Julianne had good energy together. Shirley saw the potential and offered to take her to London with us.

At first, neither Julianne nor my parents were too interested. But I was a good salesman: "I had a great time—you'll love it!" I vouched for Shirley and Corky. At the end of the summer break, she relented—as did our mom and dad. Back we went, this time with Julianne in tow. It was a huge change for her, but just as I had, she adjusted quickly. She started at Italia Conti and tagged along with us on the train. She slipped into the regime of school, practice, living with the Ballases, and dancing with Mark. Friends would ask me if I minded having my best friend and sister compete against me. Strangely, I didn't. I thought they were a good match, and most of the time—because they were nine and eleven, and I was twelve—we were in different age categories. But even when we did face off, there was no bad blood. It wasn't about trying to be better than one or the other. It was about what we could bring to the table each day. We each had different strengths: What could we do to push and inspire each other? Was

THE BALLAS BRAT PACK   67

there some new step I picked up in practice? A new song that Mark heard that we could try out on the guitar and drums? We all shared the same goals and purpose, so it united us. I wanted them to win as much as I wanted it for myself. I went from being the fourth youngest in a family of five to the oldest brother of three. It was a big identity shift for me, and I was very protective of both of them.

That said, Julianne was definitely a competitor—maybe more than even I was. She loved to brag about how she could beat me (for the record, it only happened once!). She had something to prove being the youngest, and I had something to prove as well: that my decision to stay in London was the right one. How could it not be? I had friends, I was in school (and staying there), I had a strong structure and routine in my life. I couldn't picture going back to the way it had been before.

I remember one holiday break when I was in the car with my dad, arguing with him about staying in London. "But Dad," I pleaded, "I want to be successful."

He looked at me sternly. "You don't think I'm successful? I have beautiful kids, a home, a great job." I didn't mean to put him on the defense, and I realized that his definition of success and mine were two very different things. He didn't need fame or money or trophies to feel successful. But to me, success was being a champion. I couldn't put into words back then how I felt, but I can now. London was such a vast, culturally rich city, and I felt connected to that energy. Utah felt small and limited to me for what I wanted to achieve. They were two worlds, so very far apart.

He might not have agreed with me, but it was hard for my dad to argue with our success overseas. When it came down to it, he saw how badly I wanted to stay, and being the unselfish guy he is, he put aside his wants and his needs for mine. My mom struggled with it as well. She would be very supportive to me ("Yes, yes! Go, go!"), but behind closed doors, it would hurt her being away from her kids for so long. People thought my parents were crazy to let us go off and live with strangers. My mom got the brunt of it. They insinuated that she was a terrible mother. "How could you let them go?" nosy neighbors would ask her. She'd reply, "How could I not? How selfish would I be to stand in the way of my children's dreams?" It was very brave of her and I love her for it. In her mind, it was all about us; it always was.

My relationship with my parents changed drastically when I went to London. It had to; with an eight-hour time difference, it was difficult to connect on the phone, and when we did, I kept everything light and positive. If I had problems or concerns, I couldn't admit it to them. I didn't want them to ever worry. But I knew that when I did hit times when I was down or overwhelmed and homesick for the Utah sun, I could pick up the phone and come home the next day. I never did, but I knew the door was always wide open.

And that's what helped me stay so long—nearly ten years. Knowing that I had two homes, two lives, and two families helped me feel secure. I went from feeling like the rug had been swept out from under me to feeling that I had a strong, solid foundation on both sides of the pond. I felt like the luckiest kid in the world.

LEADING LESSONS
Live in a state of gratitude.

When I was a little boy, my dad taught us how to pray. We'd give thanks for meals; in church we'd thank God for his blessings. But as we grow older, expressing gratitude seems less important. We're not as appreciative of the little things; we lose sight of what we already have in our quest to have more. I'm not a religious person anymore, but I see the value in prayer. It's a brilliant incantation you deliver at any time during the day. You physically change your body—you fold your arms, you bow your head—and then you give thanks out loud for all that's good in your life while expressing faith that what's bad will get better. Gratitude reminds us to not give up, to have a positive attitude, and to open our hearts. When I was in London, I would gaze out the train window and think to myself, How lucky am I? Not every kid gets to follow his passion with every fiber of his being. I was so grateful, and that made everything I experienced so much richer. Today, in the crazy rush that is my life and my career, I constantly have to remind myself to stop and take stock.

Remind yourself where you come from.

I spent the majority of my life running away from Utah, from the life I led there, from the memories I associated with those early years. It felt very someone-else-ago to me. London changed me profoundly.

When we were dancing on *DWTS* together, Jennifer Grey called me one night. She was having trouble with her back and wanted to see a physiotherapist. "Can you come with me?" she asked. She drove us through a residential section of Beverly Hills. We pulled into a house with a shed out back. Oddly, it didn't look like a doctor's office. There was a couch and incense burning. An Australian guy with a white beard came in: "Hey, mates." I looked at Jen and she winked at me. This was no physical therapy. She'd signed us up for some bizarre couples therapy!

The guy spoke to us for a while, then he asked Jennifer if she wouldn't mind leaving us to chat. I thought the whole thing was pretty out there, but I didn't think I could make a run for it.

"So, Derek," he said. "Tell me about your childhood." I laid it all out for him—I talked for almost two hours—and he nodded. "You can go pick him up now."

I raised an eyebrow. "Pick who up?"

The therapist smiled. "That younger boy, that self you left in

Utah. You left him there while you've been on a mission moving forward so vigorously. Now you can go get him back."

I sat there, utterly stunned and speechless. It was beyond powerful and enlightening. Had I really left that part of me behind? Had I lost that fun-loving, wide-eyed kid and all his creative exuberance?

When I came out of my therapy session, Jennifer was waiting for me. "If I'd told you this was where we were going, you wouldn't have come," she said. She was right. She had to blindside me to get me to grapple with this. She's a very spiritual person, and she saw how I was struggling, how I seemed to be in some kind of emotional rut. Just visualizing myself taking the old Derek by the hand was an incredible exercise. I think we often tuck our younger selves away for safekeeping. In my case, I associated my early years with painful memories. I wanted to keep young Derek at a distance. But what I forgot was all the good I experienced with him as well: the joy, the hope, the excitement, the wonder. I forgot what a great kid Derek was. I gave myself permission to reconnect with that little boy, to see the world through his eyes again. It was the kick in the butt I needed.

Jennifer would say, "Told ya so."

REFLECTING ON DEREK

"In every dance that I did with Derek, there were at least two moves or moments that I looked forward to, like a kid in a candy shop. It was always very satisfying to see Derek's face after the dance was over, when he looked at me with so much pride. He and I both knew how hard-won it was. There was not a dance that we did that was easy for me. Every week, I had a crisis of faith. I could set my watch to it. Feeling like, This is the time, this is the dance where I am goin' down. Derek's brilliant choreography coupled with the experience of being taught by him was extraordinary. He is an amazing dance partner. Facing my fears in doing *Dancing with the Stars* took everything I had, and Derek made it more than worth the Herculean effort."

—JENNIFER GREY

8

WILD THANG

I'VE ALWAYS HAD this split personality: the crazy, wild, silly kid, and the very disciplined, focused dancer. My old coach Rick dubbed me "Heavy D"—that was me at my most competitive and aggressive. In London, Mark and I were a dangerous duo: crazy meets crazy. We threw Shirley's garden hose into the heated swimming pool pretending to "slay the snake." We set up a trampoline next to that pool and did flips and dives into it for hours. At Halloween, we egged houses and decorated our own to look like something out of a horror flick. I was always "borrowing" Corky's things: an Armani tux worth thousands for a school play, and his brand-new expensive Bally shoes for skateboarding. When I returned them to him, the shiny loafers looked like they had been run over by a truck.

In Utah, my parents didn't know how to punish me for misbehaving; Shirley, however, was a master at it. She knew I would spend twenty minutes every morning gelling my hair into place. All she had to do was take that gel away and I would suffer miserably! Another time, Shirley and Corky actually took the door off our room. The absence of privacy made us nuts, but it didn't stop us from acting up. When we were barely teenagers, Mark and I cruised around our posh neighborhood on our skateboards dressed in baggy jeans and hoodies.

We got chased out of any respectable place of business and run off the sidewalks for grinding on them. We got lots of dirty looks. If there was a DO NOT ENTER sign it was an open invitation for us to barge right in. We thought we were the Untouchables. We went to the local church and climbed up on the roof till we reached the steeple, laughing at the world below us. Then we sat there, daring each other not to fall off, watching the sun set.

We hung out in the newsagents' (what Americans call convenience stores), buying nothing, flipping through magazines, ogling pretty girls who wouldn't give us the time of day, until the owners tossed us out for loitering. We mouthed off to everyone and listened to no one. I think it was our way of dealing with all the discipline and structure of the dancing. If we could cut loose and act like metalheads when we weren't in rehearsal, then we wouldn't resent the long hours and hard work when we were.

I started smoking, too—I couldn't have been much older than thirteen. I found it comforting while I was waiting for a train, and I thought it made me look cool and older. One day, I was smoking with some schoolmates in the sixth-floor bathroom instead of going to class. The door to the stall was locked, and I was standing on the toilet seat, dropping my ashes out the small window, when the headmaster walked in. I thought he'd explode and suspend us—I was used to this kind of reaction back home when I misbehaved. But instead, he just chased us out with a warning. Lucky for me, my school in London was forgiving.

But this wasn't the case at home. As I mentioned, if you crossed Shirley, you paid a price. One night, around midnight, I snuck into the bathroom and lit up a cigarette. I opened the window wide and leaned my head out so no one would smell it. There was a knock at the door.

"Derek? Are you in there?" It was Shirley.

I panicked, tossed the butt out the window, and tried to fan the smell of smoke out of the room with a towel.

Finally, I opened the door. She had a stern look on her face, and I pretended I didn't notice.

"Are you smoking?" she asked.

"Huh? Smoking? No, of course not!"

Shirley stood there, glaring at me. I didn't know what she was waiting for or what else she wanted me to say.

"Are you smoking?" she repeated. Her voice was calm and low.

"No, no," I insisted. "Honest."

She raised her hand and slapped it hard across my cheek. I swear I almost swallowed my teeth.

"What the hell?" I gasped. My cheek stung and I was in shock. I could feel the five fingerprints across my face.

"That wasn't for smoking. That was for lying," she replied. Then she turned and walked back to her bedroom, shutting the door behind her.

That was the day I learned never to lie to Shirley. She could put up with just about anything—my mouth, my antics, even my smoking. But she would not tolerate anyone lying to her face. If she asked me a question, she expected an honest answer. I respected her for that, and I tried to abide by it. But sometimes, circumstances were beyond my control.

One night I was out drinking in a pub with friends. I was a teenager, and we were tossing back beers and acting like big shots. All of a sudden, the room started spinning.

"Hey, I'm taking off," I told my friends. "I don't feel great."

I stumbled out of the bar to King's Cross station to catch the train home.

I felt kind of woozy and drunk, drunker than I should have been from a few beers. I remember thinking, Someone must have spiked my drink, just as everything went black.

I woke up on the floor of the station with a homeless dude looming over me.

"Hey, pal, got some money?" he asked. His breath reeked of alcohol, but I suppose mine didn't smell much better.

I was still disoriented but managed to crawl to my feet and stumble outside, where I found a cab. I told the driver my address. I rolled down the car window and threw up the entire drive home. I was such a mess, I couldn't even make it to the front door. I collapsed in the front yard, facedown in the rain and the mud, till six in the morning.

When I finally walked into the house, Shirley was crying and Corky was furious. They had been worried sick about me all night. I prepared myself for a verbal lashing, but there was none. Just a simple order: "Take a shower and get ready for school."

My head was pounding and the smell of breakfast on the table made me want to retch. But I did as I was told. There was no missing classes because I made some stupid choice to go out and party. The Ballases taught me to own my decisions—the good, the bad, even the idiotic. I would never learn to be a man unless I took responsibility for my actions. If I had to suffer through a heinous hangover, maybe that lesson would sink in a little quicker.

When I got to school, the headmaster took pity on me. "Go take a nap in the boys' changing room," he told me. "You look awful." Trust me—I felt a hell of a lot worse than I looked.

Whenever Shirley was away, Mark and I would take full advantage. One day, we "borrowed" her BMW X5 and took it for a joyride. We thought we got away with it, till some store clerk remarked to her, "I didn't know your boys drove! I saw them driving around yesterday."

Shirley came home and was determined to get to the bottom of it.

She knew better than to ask us—we'd have some lame excuse. So she went right to Julianne. She knew she could crack her.

"Did Derek and Mark take my car?" she asked.

Jules didn't even hesitate: "Yes! And they were smoking, too!"

Mark and I stood there, our mouths hanging open. Not only had she told on us, she'd offered more details than were even asked! We got an earful from Shirley, but that wasn't all. She asked a family friend who'd been in jail several times to pay us a visit. He had a reputation for beating people up and breaking their fingers for information.

"You think that's clever? You think that's funny?" he asked us about our joyride in a super Cockney accent. The dude was a true British gangster. "If you do it again, I'll pay you another visit—and I promise it won't be pleasant." That was enough to put the fear of God in us, and we promised we'd never do it again (till next time!).

If I was going to break any rules, I had to do so without killing myself or winding up in jail. There was a way to do it on the dance floor, and Corky showed me how. When he'd started dancing with Shirley, he was a novice, and everyone in the dance community teased Shirley about partnering with him. "Why are you dancing with this guy?" they'd ask her. "He's terrible. He's not a natural dancer." But he defied them—and the odds. He didn't give a damn what people thought or said, and Shirley had an incredible faith in him and in their partnership. They knew that he had something within him. When I look back, Corky was one of the first who showed me what a true leader does. He holds his head high, he pushes past his limits, he stares down the haters and proves them all wrong.

I always improvised during dance competitions, just as I'd been taught at Center Stage by Rick. He explained that to defy the rules for the sake of defying them is a bad choice. It's about finding the right moment to interject yourself and your personality into the performance. That's when the rules can take a backseat. Some dances you need to be precise and reverent of the foundation—like a waltz. Others, you have some room to give it "flair" and your own individual character—like a jive or a samba. It made sense to me. I couldn't just go wild on the dance floor. I needed to always be in control of my body and the situation. But occasionally, my youthful exuberance got the best of me. When I was sixteen, we were at the UK championships in the Winter Gardens back in Blackpool. My partner and I were traveling clockwise around the floor doing a paso doble. I was really into it, envisioning myself as the fierce matador. I was intense. I paid no mind to what was going on around me—not the forty other dancers swirling around us, not the flow of the traffic. I thought to myself, "Man! I am on fire!" Then I heard a voice over the microphone:

"Derek, you're going the wrong way."

I froze in my tracks. It was Bill Irvine, the world champion and ballroom legend who was a commentator that day. Out of the corner of my eye I saw Corky waving his arms in the air like a madman, signaling me to turn around.

I was mortified, but I didn't want to show it. So I smiled, pretended I wasn't the least bit embarrassed, and did a 360, pulling my partner with me. I went right back into the routine, unfazed. Corky always taught me both to be quick on my feet and to think quickly. And if I screwed up, to cover my tracks.

LEADING LESSONS
Embrace your multiple personalities.

As a kid, I went back and forth between being a metalhead and a Latin dancer. A strange combination? Yes, but it showed me that I should never let one single thing define who I am. I am many things, many voices, many personalities. I try to embrace them rather than suppress them. There's a time to be disciplined and there's a time to let go. There's a time to crowd-surf and a time to practice. The more variety in your life, the more color.

Sometimes I think we give ourselves a label: "I'm an accountant." Or "I'm a mom." Or "I'm a schoolteacher." That isn't all of you, just like dancing wasn't—and still isn't—all of me. Give yourself permission to embrace all the facets of you; it's what makes you unique and special. We are who we tell ourselves we are. When I danced with Maria Menounos, she was known as an entertainment journalist and *Extra* host. But she was determined to prove there was more to her than meets the eye. So she took on *Dancing with the Stars* and added "ballroom dancer" to her résumé. That alone was impressive, but she wasn't going to stop there. For years, she's been a huge fan of wrestling and the WWE. She decided she wanted to do WrestleMania in Miami. Her agents and her managers were begging her to reconsider: "You're not a wrestler, don't do it!" Maria stood her ground: "I love it. I've always wanted to do it, and I *am* going to do it." She got smacked but also smacked down her opponents. The woman is tough! She never lets herself get pigeonholed into one identity. She's striving and seeking more—which is what leaders do. Don't be afraid to call yourself many different names. I like being both Derek and Heavy D—and you ain't seen nothing yet.

Lies always hurt.

Shirley made it clear to me that she would accept nothing but 100 percent honesty in our relationship. That slap across the face was an eye-opener. It made me feel that I didn't need to sneak around behind her back. It gave me the freedom for the first time in my life to let go of my secrets. It's a lesson that I continue to learn—if you lie, no matter how good your intentions, you carry the lie with you. It weighs you down, it holds you back, and you start to lose respect for yourself.

The biggest lies of all are those we tell ourselves. Every time you say, "I can't do that," "I don't have what it takes," "It's too late," or "I'm not good enough," you're keeping yourself from living your truth. This is always a tough one for me, and something I continually have to work on. Why do we lie to ourselves? Because a lie feels easy and comfortable. It keeps fear and pain away; it shields you from the unknown. But you deserve more. You deserve not to settle, not to be distracted, and not to deny yourself your highest potential. As the saying goes, "The truth shall set you free." Be honest about what you want, what you need, and what you're capable of. Tune out the negative voices in your head that hold you back. Change your mind, change yourself.

You create your reality.

Corky reinforced this idea for me. He believes that even when you're not feeling on top of your game, you need to tell yourself that you are and put that image out there. It's like shifting a gear from off to on. If you are not feeling happy or driven, then make an effort to radiate a sense of confidence. If you're mortified that you screwed up a dance, pretend you're proud and unfazed. It's not self-deception; it's creating your own reality. Put it out there in the universe and watch what happens. You begin to realize who you are is what you believe you are. Your personal perception of reality is determined by how you think and feel. Your thoughts and feelings create your attitude, and your attitude dictates how you act. We all have an incredible power at our disposal: the power to become what we think about. Visualize what you want. See it, own it, be it.

REFLECTING ON DEREK

"I was never a dancer. My parents couldn't afford recitals and other dance-related activities. On top of that, I was born with crooked legs and still have an awkward style of running to this day. And yet, with two broken feet and broken ribs, on *Dancing with the Stars,* I made it to the semifinals and beat the other finalists' score. There was only one reason I was able to do it, and that was Derek. He is simply the best combination of choreographer, dancer, and teacher in the world. I don't say that because he is my friend. I say it because it's true, and if you don't see it season after season on *Dancing with the Stars* then I don't know what you are watching. Derek is a sensitive being, a creative genius, and a natural storyteller. When you incorporate those elements into teaching, along with the deepest knowledge of technique and craft, you can't help but come out a winner."

—MARIA MENOUNOS

Chubby!

Holy sombrero! If anyone has seen this hat, please return it to me immediately. I need it back!

My first encounter with a drum—I was already drawn to a good beat!

We were always an outdoor kind of family.

My karate class—one of the many activities that I hated going to and ended up loving.

Our family in Temple Square in Salt Lake City.

My dance partner Autumn and I in 1997 standing proudly
with one of our many trophies.

Winning first place in the Juniors age group at Blackpool in 1998 with Leanne
Noble. My first big win!

Jade and me. Puppy love!

Goofing off with the Center Stage gang and my partner Autumn DelGrosso.

Me and my mom— check out those biceps . . . or lack thereof!

Sporting my Dallas Cowboys gear. Little did I know that one day I'd be dancing alongside Emmitt Smith!

Hanging with Jules in the desert— my love of being outdoors started early.

Ballas family portrait from 2000— Julianne and I were always included and made to feel like part of the family.

I had just climbed the Grand Teton Mountains in Wyoming. Don't look down!

All smiles at my sister Marabeth's wedding.

The Hough sibs partying at my sister Katherine's wedding.

My niece Arianna and me: I love being Uncle D.

Dad's got his wild and crazy side, too. This is where I got it from!

Turkey Day fun with my sisters.

Moments before he took me up skydiving, this dude's chute failed and he almost died. The scary part is not the actual jump—it's the seconds before it, the anticipation. That's the slap in the face.

Swimming with sharks at night in Bora Bora.

There's no business like *snow* business. . . .

I was so proud that I could help Ricki learn to love what she saw in the mirror.

Backstage with partner and Olympic gymnast Shawn Johnson during *DWTS: All-Stars*.

Me, Meryl, and Charlie. I had never choreographed on ice before—which made me want to do it even more.

With Amy Purdy in Sochi, Russia, at the 2014 Paralympic Games. It was a few days before our first live dance on *DWTS*, and we rehearsed whenever and wherever we could!

Kellie Pickler was always a lot stronger than she thought.

Nothing's going to stop Jules! Not even an injured foot on the first day of rehearsal for our Move tour.

If I don't know how I'm going to choreograph a dance, I break it down piece by piece until it takes shape. Here, I'm studying a rotating room for a gravity-defying "Macy's Stars of Dance" number.

Hanging out with Julianne. She's more than just my sister—she's one of my best friends.

Five, count 'em, five Mirror Balls. Sometimes the light from the window hits them just right and my office turns into Studio 54.

Oh yeah! We are the champions!!

Winning my first Mirror Ball—Mom couldn't help crying. Loved that moment.

As a kid, water terrified me.
Today doing something that scares me reminds me that I'm alive.

As a kid, I hated ballet and used to cut classes all the time. But Misty Copeland changed my opinion when I choreographed her. She's so strong that she makes me look like a wimp!

The quiet before the show.

Sometimes you just have to stop everything, take it all in, and let your mind rest. Here I am, hiking with my dog, Romie, and checking out the view of Runyon Canyon.

Who, me? An Emmy winner? One of the proudest and most exciting moments of my career.

9

CHANGE PARTNERS AND DANCE

AFTER YEARS OF competing, all the times you've battled it out on the ballroom dance floor start to blur together. Only a handful really stand out in my mind—some because they were huge victories, some because they were huge disappointments. But as my coaches loved to remind me, you can never go back and do it over. You can only go forward and do it better. That's the case in ballroom and in life.

I was back at Blackpool in the teen division, dancing with Leanne Noble and representing the UK. Out of the corner of my eye, during round 2 or 3, I saw this guy gliding across the floor with his partner. He had dark hair and he was bigger than me for sure. He was also a year older, which, at that age, was a lifetime. His dancing was so smooth and fluid, so controlled. I was fun and energetic, but I couldn't match his quality of movement. I knew most of the competitors, but I didn't know him, so naively, I didn't see him as a threat. My coaches, however, were sweating.

"Derek," Shirley warned me, "you're going to lose this competition if you don't pull it out." I nodded and took a deep breath. I didn't want my year's training to go to waste. So I went out danced my ass off. We were all exhausted by the final round, but I kept my energy up. Even when the song finished, I kept going. I had the crowd chanting the team number on our backs. I was totally in the zone. I wasn't even aware of what was going on around me—all I kept thinking was, "I got this. I won this finale."

They started announcing results and I was pretty confident we were going to be number 1. They went from sixth place all the way down to second and I was still standing there, waiting for our name and number. Then I heard, "In second place, Derek Hough and Leanne Noble . . ." I was devastated. I worked so hard all year and I still lost. I collected my trophy, posed for pics, then came off the floor and cried like a baby. Of course, the Russian guy came in first. I went to the judges—I needed some explanation.

"I nailed that finale," I told them. "Why didn't I win?" One judge put it succinctly: "You're right, you won the finale, but you didn't win the competition. You've got to win from the first round, from the very first moment." So I hadn't shown consistency all day. Corky patted me on the back. "You have to treat each round as if it were your last," he said. "Everything you do has to be 110 percent."

After Leanne, I had a partner named Rachael Heron. She was from Liverpool, like the Beatles, and she was the best in the world in our age group at the time. Besides dancing, we started dating as well. And when I say dating, I mean I made her a blanket with her name on it, and she gave me a bottle of cologne. We walked around holding hands and kissed a little. Ah, young love. Being with her made me up my game, because she was better than I was. But her family was very intense. We'd be competing in a ballroom competition, and her mom would stand on the sidelines screaming, "Go on, Number 54!" like it was the final seconds of the Super Bowl. She'd also scream if I did something wrong—I mean really rip into me. I think she thought it was motivating. The truth? It made me feel like a loser, despite the fact that Rachael and I won all the competitions all over Europe—France, Italy, London, we took them all. We were kicking butt. Then, out of the blue, I got a phone call: "We no longer want to dance with Derek."

They said "we" because it was basically Rachael's dad that did the dumping. He called me, not her. I wanted to know what I did wrong, but the Herons were not going to elaborate. It was more, "Don't call us, we'll call you." *Click*. It shook me up, and self-doubt started creeping into my mind. It was the first time I had to deal with someone breaking off a partnership. The Herons never said it, but the message was clear: "We think there is someone better than you and we want Rachael to dance with him."

I wanted to crawl into a hole, I was so humiliated. "You gotta get back on the horse," Corky told me. "No pity party. Prove them wrong." So I got another partner, Heidi Clarke, and we began training. Coincidentally, she had been dumped by Rachael's new partner, Rory Couper. We called ourselves "the Rejects" for a while and tried not to be too depressed. The American Open was coming up in Miami, and we had only a month and a half to prepare. Rory and Rachael would be there, and we had to show them up.

We went back to the States to train over the summer break, but I just couldn't concentrate. To be honest, whenever I practiced in America, I never got as much done or had the same hunger or drive as when I was in England. But I pushed through it, and we went to our first competition, a small one in Las Vegas. Mark and Julianne were actually competing against us, and for the first time, they beat me. I was angry at myself that we lost, and I turned that anger on my friend and my sister. I was pretty rude and obnoxious about it. "How can I beat Rachael if I can't even beat Mark and Julianne?" I whined to Shirley.

She looked at me with utter disgust. How could I not be happy for them? How could I not give them credit for what they achieved? "You're behaving like a brat," she scolded me. "Enough!"

But I was blinded by revenge; proving Rachel and her parents wrong was all I could think about. It consumed me. Mark and Julianne were relaxed and having fun on the dance floor. I was a ball of anger and insecurity. All of a sudden, dancing wasn't for me or my partner; it was for someone else who wasn't even in my life.

Shirley urged me to concentrate on the upcoming Open and forget about Rachael. I had to block it out and focus on the here and now. Easier said than done. At the time, dance competitions in America were very different from those in England. Here, it's less about quality and technique, and more about showmanship and connecting with the audience. We worked hard and the day finally arrived. It was being shown live on TV, and there were cameras everywhere. The hotel was heaving with people—competitors from all over the world.

We walked onto the dance floor and I could feel the energy in the room. I saw Rachael and held my breath for a quick second. Heidi looked at me: "You okay?"

I nodded and took my position. "Here we go," I told her.

As we started dancing, I felt run down. Maybe it was the Miami heat and sun (I'd been lying out by the pool the day before), but my stamina wasn't where it should have been. I pushed through it, and we made it into the finals. But my lungs felt like they were going to explode during the jive. I could feel my heartbeat in my face. I gave myself a last-minute pep talk: "Go for it or go home." My body was starting to shut down, but I kept kicking. When they called time, I was so exhausted, I practically crawled off the floor. We waited nervously as they tallied the results.

The announcer called sixth place, fifth place, fourth place, third place, and then second: "Rachael Heron and Rory Couper." Heidi and I looked at each other. That meant only one thing: the Rejects were first! We were jumping up and down, hugging our coaches, flying around the floor like lunatics. I wanted to run over to Rachael and rub it in her face, but I caught myself. What was the point? The victory was not in beating my ex. It was in realizing that nothing could keep me down and no disappointment could ever destroy me.

When we got back to England, there was another big competition already on our calendar. That's the way it is; you barely get a second to celebrate or breathe before it's back to the practice hall. Some of the other dancers were catty about my win in America. I heard the whispers: "They only gave it to him because he's American." There was a camp that thought Rachael and Rory should have won instead. I tried to tune it out. I knew we weren't technically the best or the most developed partnership, but I believed we had something more. My old training from Utah kicked in and I could hear Rick Robinson telling me to just work the crowd and be an entertainer: "Rip it up!"

We trained hard, for hours and hours every day. When we arrived at the competition, I felt good. I felt like we'd put in our time and we were ready to take this. Corky came over to us with some last-minute advice—he was a mastermind at the game. He pointed to Rachael and Rory. "Walk around the floor before you start to dance," he instructed me. "Go over and give them a look, intimidate them." Was this a dance competition or a fight in a boxing ring?

This wasn't at all my style, but I did it. I wondered how Rachael felt now that the tables were turned. She had something to prove this time, not me. She was the one who needed to worry. During the first round, we were practically stalking them. Normally when you are competing against someone, you want a lot of space. You'll be on opposite sides of the dance floor. But, no, I was right next to them the whole time. I wanted them to see we weren't afraid to stand next to them. I knew that they thought they were better, but I wanted to rattle them. It also got the crowd stirred up: this was going to be a showdown on the dance floor.

On the break, my other coach, Graham Oswick, came over to me. "Stop doing that," he said. "It's enough. It's not your time to win this. It's their time."

That made me furious: he just blatantly told me that I should give up and settle for second best. I went over and found Corky.

"That motherfucker!" he shouted. "Hell no, you're not giving up! We're going to intensify it. We're going to defy him and everyone else."

I could see he was pretty fired up. "Are you sure?" I asked.

He gave me a little push back onto the floor. "Do it."

So we went back out there, guns blazing. Heidi and I danced our hearts out and made it into the semifinals. We were doing the jive and she accidentally elbowed me in the face. I tasted blood and realized I had bitten down so hard on my tongue, a piece of it was literally hanging off! Blood was pumping out of my mouth, but I kept on dancing. It was dripping down my face and all over my costume; I looked like something out of a slasher flick.

When we finally finished, Corky grabbed me and raced me upstairs to a little room where I could put my head back. He tried to stop the bleeding and brought me ice to take the swelling down.

I was lying there, trying to hold my tongue together, when I heard a voice at the doorway—a voice with a Liverpudlian accent.

"Derek, stay away from me!" Rachael demanded. "Stay on your side of the floor."

I managed a weak thumbs-up and she stormed off.

"Can you hang in there?" Corky asked me. I nodded; I was afraid if I spoke my tongue would literally fall off. I changed my blood-soaked shirt and went back to the dance floor. We got to the finals, and I was still bleeding profusely. I didn't let it stop me. In between each dance, I ran to the corner of the stage to spit out puddles of blood.

We didn't have long to wait for the results. This time, they announced the winners first: "Couple number 72 from England, Derek Hough and Heidi Clark." I ran onto the floor. I couldn't believe it. Injury and all, we'd shown we were a force to be reckoned with. We were rejects no more.

LEADING LESSONS
Rejection is an illusion.

It's all in your head. It was never about Rachael; it was always about me. So maybe I didn't fit her picture of the perfect dance partner. We were no longer a match—so what? At the time, the rejection hurt like hell and I threw myself a big ol' pity party. But here's the thing: No one can reject you. No one can dump you. It's just a decision, and maybe you don't like it. I was the one believing I was a victim instead of realizing how blessed my life was. If you're feeling rejected, you're looking at things all wrong. Just because someone says no, just because someone chooses another person over you, doesn't mean you're not good enough. There isn't one successful person out there who hasn't racked up his or her share of rejection.

That said, no one likes hearing no. But what are you going to do with that no? Are you going to let it destroy your self-esteem? Or are you going to keep pushing forward, following your passion? Dancers deal with a lot of rejection—I know this now, and I see the rejections as part of my journey. Keep doing what you're doing and do it well—don't worry about pleasing anyone but yourself. Sometimes that no can be a wake-up call, a chance for you to reassess, refocus, reboot. I'm grateful Rachael and her family gave me my walking papers. That rejection opened me up to so much more.

Competition shouldn't be personal.

All the times I've focused on taking someone down, I've fallen short. Your motivation for winning has to be in the right place. Years ago, I was in a competition in London, and I really wanted to best this other couple. Why? So I could say I did. All I could think was, I'm gonna beat them. I'm gonna beat them. So I danced hard and frenzied, trying to overpower them. There was no control of my body, no light and shade in my dancing. My coaches pulled me aside: "What the hell was that?" I see now where I went wrong: I made it all about my competitors, when it should have been about my partner and me. I should have seen my competitors not as a target, but as a catalyst to inspire me to be better, stronger, and more in control. Instead, I made it a one-upping contest—and they wound up one-upping me.

Whatever you focus on is your reality.

You tend to move in the direction of what you're focused on—especially when it's bad. I remember when I was about nine years old, staying with my grandma and grandpa at the lake, I was playing with my cousins at this construction site. Not the safest place to play, which I suppose is what attracted me to it. I saw a two-by-four with a nail sticking out of it, and I remember running and thinking, Oh man, wouldn't it be terrible if I fell on that? A few moments later, it actually happened. I tripped and the nail went straight through my knee. I ended up going to the hospital with a two-by-four stuck to my knee because we were afraid to pull it out. The nail was about a centimeter away from cutting a vital tendon that would have required major surgery. So I was really fortunate in that regard. But I couldn't help thinking that my focus on this nail created the situation. I've learned since then that we all have the power to create our own destiny. On some level, we ask for things that happen to us in our lives. You have to know what you want, then be aware of the thoughts you hold in your mind. Negative ones—fear, anger, jealousy, frustration—will undermine you. If you see the nail tripping you up, it will.

REFLECTING ON DEREK

"Derek was so young when we danced together back in Season 7—I was his third partner. He was finding his way; he hadn't won his first Mirror Ball yet. He was so different than he is now, in such a sweet and vulnerable way. I don't think he knew how truly talented he was back then. But he always had this magical ability to make people great. From the tips of my fingers to the bottom of my toes, nothing was ever good enough until it was perfect. Neither of us ever expected to win Season 7. When we did our freestyle, we never ran it through from beginning to end. I was injured; Derek threw out his back. Even in dress rehearsals we barely did it. When it came time to go out and perform, we stood backstage and looked at each other, hoping for the best. It had so many tricks, and we kind of surprised ourselves with how well we nailed it. Fast-forward five years, and I see how many life lessons I've learned from my friend Derek. He helped me discover my own champion. He taught me how to dance through chaos, and how to find my own rhythm in my everyday life. I feel like we did a lot of growing and learning together."

—BROOKE BURKE

10

THE WORLD IN MY HANDS

A FTER HEIDI, I partnered with Aneta Piotrowska. She was a knockout: a beautiful, exotic Polish girl with long dark hair. She was sixteen and I was seventeen, and of course, I had an instant crush on her. I'm not even sure how we first met—probably through recommendations from dance coaches who thought we'd be good together. We started dancing together in 2002 and were partners for more than two years. She was my first foreign partner—before I had been only with English girls. I loved her energy and her cute Polish accent.

Aneta and I were dancing at a qualifying competition in Poland for the World Under 21 Latin Championships. Shirley and Corky decided that we should represent Poland, since it gave us the best chance of making the worlds. It was a calculated political move: the American and UK judges knew who I was, but I needed to catch the eye of the European judges. Representing Poland was the easiest way. To compete, you had to place in the top two of your country. I agreed to it all, although it was definitely weird not to be representing the United States or England, and I barely understood a word of Polish.

In the first round of the first dance, at about nine in the morning, we were doing the cha-cha and getting ready to transition to the samba. We were really into it, what I like to call being "in the zone," when Aneta accidentally elbowed me in the face with such force that she knocked me out.

I woke up on the floor with Corky leaning over me. "Are you okay? I'm sorry!" Aneta said. There was no time for apologies or for me to even get my bearings. We had already missed an entire samba dance in our heat while I was unconscious, and the rumba was next. I stumbled to my feet and took her hand on the dance floor, but my jaw was swollen and throbbing. The medic injected some numbing cream into it, so as the pain faded I began to drool. I felt like I had just gotten a filling at the dentist. There we were, doing this sexy Latin dance of love, and saliva was dribbling down my chin! As I danced, I noticed the drool flying everywhere—onto Aneta, onto the other couples dancing, onto the dance floor. It would have been pretty hilarious had I not been such a nervous wreck worrying that we would blow it. But when they announced the winner, we came in first—even with my round 1 knockout.

We had a couple of months to get ready for the worlds. We went back to London, our home base to train, and I decided in between practices to lift some weights in the makeshift gym I had set up in our one-car garage. I was nineteen at the time, trying to build up the pecs on one side of my chest. So I stupidly put a heavy weight on one side and it threw the whole dumbbell off-balance. The weight slipped out of my hands and fell. I felt a shooting pain rip through my neck.

When I woke up in the morning I was in bad shape. My neck was stiff and I couldn't turn it. We weren't pros, so there was so such thing as a physical therapist or masseuse to fix it. The best I could do was just rub in some Bengay and hope for the best. When we got to the Czech Republic a couple of days later, my neck still had zero mobility. In order to look to the side, I had to move my entire body. As if that weren't enough to worry about, we were competing against Rachael, who was now teamed up with the Russian guy who had beaten me as a junior. His name was Evgeni Smagin, and he wore his dark hair greased back. The guy just looked slick from head to toe.

I turned to Aneta. "This is so not good," I told her. "They are like the ultimate, *ultimate* couple. They're going to beat us."

Aneta looked very upset, so I guess something inside me said, "Derek, man up!" My neck was messed up and I was about to get my ass kicked by my archnemesis and my ex. It couldn't get much worse than that. But we were at the worlds, in this huge arena with everyone cheering. We had made it this far, and I was proud of how hard we worked. "You know, let's just have an awesome time."

And that was it: I took all this pressure off us. We danced our butts off and I forgot to worry about my neck or Rachael and Evgeni. I was just living in the moment, pulling my energy from the roaring crowd. They were going crazy for their Czech Republic representatives, but I didn't care. I used their energy to fuel mine. There was such a joy and freedom to my dancing that day. I gave myself permission to just let it all go, and my dancing felt pure and unbridled. We got to the finale—I somehow hung in there—and my neck was so tight and throbbing, I could barely turn it to see where Aneta was. It was kind of like dancing with blinders on; I had tunnel vision. Yet on we danced, till the judges called time. I had made it; we had made it. All I wanted now was a huge ice pack and a nap.

They read the names out from sixth place to first. We were standing backstage behind a huge curtain, and Rachael and Evgeni were right next to us. Swell. I thought maybe we stood a chance of coming in fourth. But they didn't call us. "This is crazy!" I whispered to

Aneta. "We're top three?" Then they called a German couple. We were in the top two!

Rachael smiled at me. "Oh, Derek! Great job!" she said. What she really meant was, "We're going to take first place and you can have our sloppy seconds." Then we heard, "In second place, from England . . ." Rachael's face went white as a ghost. She and Evgeni were second! That left only one place for us . . .

"Derek Hough and Aneta Piotrovska are world champions!"

I started screaming, "What? What?" and jumping up and down. So much for my neck pain. This wasn't real; it couldn't be! I ran out from behind the curtain, pumping my fists in the air. I caught a glimpse of Rachael's face. She was beyond pissed.

"We did it! We did it!" I yelled. The rest happened in slow motion: I ran out and jumped off the stage, not realizing there were about fourteen steps between the stage and the floor. While I was midair, I remember thinking, "I'm wearing these Cuban heels. This isn't gonna be good." Then I hit the floor and my legs buckled. I fell into a roll, then stood straight up—as if I meant to do it all along. I limped over to Aneta to collect our trophy and we hugged. I didn't give a crap about anything else. Not my neck or my knees or Rachael fuming as they snapped pictures of all of us. It was an amazing moment, a total high.

The next day, we were driving back to Poland to catch a flight to London. I was barely paying attention when we decided to stop at Auschwitz, the Holocaust death camp. I hadn't learned a thing about the Holocaust in school, so I had no idea what this place was. I remember it was raining, and the sky was filled with dark storm clouds. We walked through the chambers, viewing the collections of personal effects that had belonged to the people who were killed here. There were piles and piles of shoes, glasses, prayer books. We surveyed the rooms in silence. What could you say? The pain these people had to endure was unfathomable. Why? What had they done? Nothing.

The numbers were devastating: millions of innocent people killed, torn from their families, treated like animals, not human beings.

I realized in that moment how lucky I was. I wanted to drop to my knees and thank the universe for everything I had: my family, the Ballases, my life in London. My win felt so insignificant at this moment. The experience definitely planted a seed in my mind: life is so precious, you can't waste a single moment of it on frivolous thoughts or actions.

Years later, my dad gave me a book to read: *Man's Search for Meaning*, by Viktor Frankl. I thought it would be depressing given the subject matter, but it wasn't. Frankl believed that you should identify a purpose in life to feel positively about, then actively imagine that outcome. It was how so many people survived the ordeal of the concentration camps. He made it his mission to inspire his fellow prisoners and keep them focused: together, they composed speeches, reconstructed lost manuscripts, pushed away any thoughts of suicide. They clung fervently to the hope of what the future held—despite the odds, despite the fact that everything around them was bleak.

I felt enlightened; I couldn't put the book down. Frankl's words struck a chord deep inside me. What he was saying was that no matter the trials and tribulations you are forced to endure, you and you alone have the power to survive. One section in particular stayed with me: he wrote about being in a car on the train tracks en route to Auschwitz. It was freezing cold, with snow on the ground outside and bodies packed into the cars. But when he woke up, there was a beautiful sunset on the horizon. Even though Frankl was in hell, he knew there was beauty out there and that no one could take that away from him.

What had started as the greatest high in my life—winning the world championships—became so much more. My trip was a turning point, the first step in this man's search for meaning.

LEADING LESSONS
There's always an answer.

No problem is ever hopeless—not even when you're facing your ene-mies with a stiff neck! With every disappointment on the dance floor, I grew to believe this more. Now, instead of feeling overwhelmed, frazzled, or that life is conspiring against me, I hold on and tell myself the answer is just an inch away. Great leaders are great sim-plifiers. They can cut through the doubt and despair so the solution becomes clear. It may not be instantaneous, but it will be there. Every challenge can be faced in dozens of ways. Sometimes the situation changes, or sometimes you change the way you see the situation. Part of our human condition is that we feel that we have to suffer in order to solve a problem. It doesn't have to be this way. Sometimes surren-der is freedom.

You always have the power of choice.

Externally, things may be out of your control. But one thing you can always control and master is your inner control: how you perceive the situation, how you filter it. There's a tremendous freedom in taking leadership of how you perceive things. An obstacle is only an obstacle if that's how you look at it. We make choices every day, and when you choose *not* to choose you are also making a choice. As soon as you make the conscious decision to be happy or successful, the universe moves to get you there. You can choose what impacts you. You can choose what scares you. You can choose to be confident, loved, or damaged. You can choose to let something define you or nothing define you. You can't change the cards you were dealt, but you can always choose how you play your hand.

Visualize a purpose and an outcome.

This concept really struck me from reading Frankl, and it's a lesson all leaders need to master. Think of it as a mental dress rehearsal for what will happen (notice I said *will*, not could). If you picture a positive result, it trains your brain to look for the resources that will help you achieve it. Seeing what you want stimulates your creativity and strengthens your confidence. This is more than just daydreaming. It's eliminating the self-doubt and negativity that can deter you, and putting in place a plan that will lead you on your desired path. And once you know that there's a light at the end of the tunnel, it's much easier to face the dark.

REFLECTING ON DEREK

"Derek was taught from a young age to have an open mind and to use out-of-the-box thinking. I am very proud that this still continues in his life; it makes all the difference."

—CORKY BALLAS

11

CUTTING FOOTLOOSE

WHEN I GOT back from winning the worlds, I felt like something had shifted inside me. I did some more competitions for a while, but the fire was starting to die down. I couldn't believe that I would ever stop wanting to win; competing had been my whole life up until now, and I didn't know I was capable of wanting anything else. But when I reached my goal, I thought it would feel different—that the thrill would last me a lifetime. Instead, I felt itchy. What could I do to challenge myself now? What else was there for me to do besides compete? Had I plateaued at nineteen?

Shirley and Corky supported my decision to do something different 100 percent. They never wanted Mark, Julianne, or me to make a life out of being a competitive dancer. To them, it was a stepping-stone, a means to achieving more. They were just as eager as I was to see what the next chapters of my life would hold. I had some definite ideas. I had always loved singing—even if it was just with Mark—and I had back-burnered it because of my dancing. I'd dabbled in musical theater in school. Italia Conti was always putting on some show or another: *Miss Saigon, Jekyll & Hyde, The Wild Party, Chess.* I was even the lead, Cliff, in the school production of *Cabaret.* So I got a head shot and put together a résumé and decided to go on some real auditions. I did three or four competitions at the same time and didn't win. It became clear to me that I couldn't do both. If I wanted to be in musicals, then that had to get 100 percent of my attention. So I stopped training and competing and put all my energy into theater.

While I was well known in the ballroom dance community, no one had ever heard of me in the theater circles. I was a kid with no experience and not a clue of how the process even worked. It was like starting with a clean slate and having to prove myself all over again. There were plenty of rejections (too short; too tall; too young; too inexperienced; too blond!), before I wound up as a background dancer—literally, the last guy on the left in the back—in *Chitty Chitty Bang Bang.* The show was playing at the world famous London Palladium in Oxford Circus, and it was my first real paying job—a couple hundred pounds a week. It was anything but glamorous: ten guys all crammed into one tiny changing room.

When I was hired, they asked me to cut my hair so I could look more like everyone else in the ensemble. I refused; long hair was kind of my thing. Instead, I gelled it and hair-sprayed it down so tightly, hurricane-force winds wouldn't have been able to budge it. Thankfully, they didn't complain or fire me. They had bigger things to worry about—like how to make a magical car fly over the stage. The whole show was pretty hokey and so not me, but it was an amazing learning experience and it lit that fire in me again. The guy I sat next to in the dressing room had been in theater for twenty years. He was about thirty-eight, and he was always picked for the same parts in the chorus. I looked at him, and the prospect of being in his shoes twenty years later terrified me. I didn't want to be that. I didn't want to spend my life going from show to show and never progressing. It was always the case with me: whenever I started something, I couldn't rest until I became the best at it. A chorus boy job was fine for right now, but I had bigger dreams. I wanted not only to sing and dance in the West End—I wanted to be a lead.

After the show ended, I auditioned for *Fame: The Musical*. Like most cattle calls, it was held in a dark, dingy, old building. There were about twenty people hanging out in the hallways, warming up. I went into the bathroom to run through my song—at least it was quiet in there. I waited a few hours for them to call me in.

"So, what are you going to do for us, Derek?"

I handed the piano player a rumpled piece of sheet music. " 'One Song Glory,' from *Rent*." It was my go-to audition song. I loved the lyrics and the idea behind it: time flies, find one song that rings true and brings you glory. They asked me to read a scene from the show, and while Karen Bruce, the choreographer, seemed to like me, in the end I didn't get the part. A few weeks after, I went on an audition for *Footloose*. There was Karen again; she was both the choreographer and director this time. I read for the part of Ren (if you're the one person on the planet who hasn't seen the 1984 movie, that's the Kevin Bacon part). They asked me to read a scene opposite this short stocky guy named Giovanni Spano who was playing Ren's right-hand man, Willard. He was a total ball of energy with a Cockney accent, and we became instant friends.

I had no idea, but after Karen saw me at the *Fame* audition, she was thinking of me for this role. I could really connect with the character, a rebel living in a small, religious town who has a passion for dancing. It could have easily been my life story. The original movie was actually shot in Utah, about fifteen miles from where we lived, and they filmed a scene in the Old Mill right near my old dance studio. I was convinced it was fate.

But it took a lot more convincing for the producers to hire me. I was called back over and over. I could almost read their minds as they watched me act out a scene or sing one of the songs: "This kid is so green. Can he really carry a show?" In the end, they gave me the chance. I was too excited to realize how unprepared I was for all of this. Most people take years to work their way up to a lead. I was just thrown into it. I didn't have a clue what I was getting myself into. Everyone in the cast and creative team warned me that the role was very physically demanding, more than most roles in the West End. "Pace yourself," they said. "If you don't, you'll never last for the four shows on the weekend."

But I didn't know how to tone it down. Ballroom is all about hitting everything full-on, giving 110 percent from start to finish. I remember I was in the middle of rehearsing "I Can't Stand Still"— strutting around the stage, doing flips and dips, and I was so out of breath I could barely sing. I was not hitting my notes and I was struggling.

Karen looked nervous. "We have to work this out," she told me. Translation: get it together or we're going to have to replace you with someone who can. When we took a two-week break for the holidays, I went home to Utah but didn't go on vacation with the rest of my family. Instead, I stayed home for Christmas and sang all my *Footloose* songs while sprinting on the treadmill. It was the only way I could learn to get control of my breath and bring my heart rate down. It was intense, but it was what I had to do to build up my stamina. I felt like I was training for a marathon. The responsibility of carrying the show weighed heavily on my shoulders. I didn't want to let anyone down. I didn't want the show to flop because I couldn't cut it.

When I got back to London, I was ready. I had learned all my lines and songs, and I could sing standing on my head if I needed to. I remember Karen's face lighting up: "Okay, now we got something. We made the right decision."

When the show started, I also started taking voice lessons. I noticed that by the end of the week, my voice would start to thin out. I went to this famous voice coach, Mary Hammond. She was a friendly redheaded lady, and she has taught practically everyone in West End theater as well as a handful of pop and rock singers. One afternoon I walked into her studio just as Chris Martin from Coldplay was walking out. She taught me to always focus on my breath—no matter where I was, I would practice breathing in and breathing out, inflating my diaphragm and controlling the inhale and exhale so they were smooth and sustained. In the beginning, I had to constantly think about the technique. But eventually, it became second nature. I was training my breath just as I had trained my body for dance. The more I practiced, the better I got at it.

We toured first before settling in at the Novello Theatre on the Strand. When you tour in England, it's nothing fancy. I was in charge of my own travel and accommodations. Sometimes I stayed in RVs or in little flats. One time I bunked in some old lady's house surrounded by her cats. I can't even remember the names of some of the cities we played in. It was all a blur, and I tried to get into the rhythm of eight shows a week. It was relentless and grueling and very different from the life I had known as a competitive dancer. I didn't miss competing at all; what I missed was the ritual and structure of it. There was always a clear goal, a deadline, a buildup, then the satisfaction in knowing it was over and done with. In live theater, you hope and pray the show doesn't open and close the same night. You hope it has a long run with no end in sight. I had never experienced that feeling—competing is more hit and run. It took some getting used to.

Opening night, all three Ballases were there. Shirley and Corky were surprised at how strong my voice was: they knew I could dance, but this was something new. Even though I was no longer a little kid, I wanted their thumbs-up. They might have been my dance coaches, but they were also my family. They never wanted me to get trapped in the world of competitive dance. They saw bigger things ahead, and this was just the beginning. Over the next few months, my entire family—my parents, sisters, grandparents—flew over to see me in the show. I actually got rave reviews from the London theater critics, but it was my family's raves that meant the most to me.

After the show, everybody would go out drinking, but I was always in bed by eleven thirty. There was no partying for me; I was the boring one. I lived in constant fear that my voice would give out on me, so I tried to rest it, eat right, get lots of sleep. I ate chicken breasts and whole potatoes like they were apples to keep up my energy and maintain my weight. When I came home after the show, Nan would leave my dinner ready and waiting in the microwave, and I would just heat it up. The Ballases always had a thing about not eating alone. Even if it was midnight, Nan would hear me banging around the kitchen, come downstairs in her robe, light up a cigarette, and keep me company. We'd chat about our day for about an hour while I ate, and it was our time together. I don't know if it's an English thing or what, but getting my Nan to say "I love you" was like pulling teeth. I came from a family where it was said often, and I was determined to teach her. So I would joke with her and grab her: "I'm not going to bed unless you say you love me back!" She would kind of mumble it, but I would insist she say it properly until she eventually caved in. I continued doing this whenever we parted ways, until eventually it became natural for her to say.

After every performance, my clothes were drenched in sweat. On matinee days, I had to take them off in the wings and put them in the dryer for the next show. There was no time to wash them! When I'd leave the stage, I'd have to go and sit down for a good ten minutes just to get my breath back. That's when I also decided it was time to kick my smoking addiction. In London, practically everyone smokes— men, women, kids. I had been smoking since I was barely a teenager—at first, to look cool, and later on because it was what everyone did. It had a feeling of community to it: we all lit up together and hung out. At least that's how I saw it back then. There was a comfort in it—the taste, the smell, the feeling of puffing on a cigarette. I couldn't imagine *not* doing it every day. It had been ingrained in me for so long.

But I realized the damage it was doing and how it was holding me back. If I smoked a pack a day, I couldn't hit the high notes. When I needed to take a deep breath, it wasn't there for me. It was preventing me from giving the best performance I knew I could give. So just like that I made a decision: no more. No agonizing, no weaning myself off, no going back. I learned in school that the word *decide* comes from the Latin word that means "to cut off." So that's what I did; I cut myself off from smoking. I trained my brain to associate the act of lighting up with pain, embarrassment, and failure. No more relaxation, no more comfort, no more camaraderie. Cigarettes became a symbol for all my anxiety. I would envision my voice cracking in front of an audience, then I'd let that feeling of humiliation and disappointment wash over me. It was the best deterrent, one that scared me a hell of a lot more than the potential health risks my family had pointed out for years. If this was what smoking might get me, I didn't want it.

So that was it. I tossed out my last pack and didn't look back. I replaced my daily smoking ritual with a new one: I drank hot herbal tea and let it coat my vocal cords and relax me. It was like I flipped a switch in my brain, turning the image of a cigarette from good to evil. Besides the physical benefits (no more wheezing; no more cracking on the high notes), I felt emotionally recharged. The high I got from beating my addiction replaced the high I got from nicotine. Even better, I did it all by myself. I made the conscious choice to break free. And when the curtain rose night after night, I never doubted I could do it. I'd beaten one of my demons, and I was ready to tackle any others that wanted to go a round with me.

LEADING LESSONS
Stretch your legs.

By this I mean you need to let go of the structure and rigidity of your life and do something different. There's a saying: You don't have to be great to start, but you have to start to be great. When I signed on to do *Footloose*, I learned about commitment on a whole new level. The tools I had called upon in the past to help me win dance competitions were not the ones I needed now. I had to find new ways to win at this as well. I had to let go of what had worked before and figure out new solutions. Flexibility is something all leaders need in their tool belt— the ability to roll with things, to shift gears, to approach something in a new and different way. The only thing certain in life is that life isn't certain. Leaders know this, expect it, and change their hearts and heads to adapt to the situation.

Addiction is a choice.

I don't care how much you think you need cigarettes, food, alcohol, drugs, whatever—the point is you are choosing to need those things. I truly believe that. You are choosing to relinquish your power and let a substance or a habit control you. To take the lead in your life, you have to decide what's important. For me, it was a no-brainer. My voice was more important to me than my need to smoke. People ask me all the time how I kicked the habit. As I wrote, I just visualized smoking as a negative; I attached that label to it and I attached pain to it. I had all these embarrassing thoughts in my head about losing my voice onstage, and smoking was always the cause of it. That was my leverage. Find yours. What is your addiction doing to hold you back? Once you align that to the addiction, it reprograms your brain. I used to smoke a pack a day, and now when I'm around someone who smokes, I can't stand the smell. I will never smoke again. But

I knew I couldn't just cut back; I had to quit cold turkey. When I found that self-discipline, my confidence soared. We often think of invoking discipline as a chore, but really, it's the ultimate freedom. It's liberating to take the power into your hands. For me the reward was complete control and freedom in the same breath.

If you want something, ask for it.

Another thing I learned while living with the Ballases was that if you want love or affection, sometimes you've just got to ask for it. This is tough for a lot of people. As adults, the fear of rejection or embarrassment often stops the words before you ever utter them. But leaders aren't afraid to ask for what they want and need. Even if someone shoots you down, you've put it out there in the universe. I'd tease Nan or Shirley: "I'm feeling kind of down today, get over here and give me a hug, dammit." And they did. The people who love you want to come through for you; you just sometimes need to make that easier by saying what you need. It isn't selfish or bossy or demanding. It's respecting yourself and your worth. I loved the freedom of not being afraid to just ask for something instead of waiting and being disappointed if it never came. Asking for something is simply the best way to ensure that you eventually get it.

REFLECTING ON DEREK

"Derek taught me to never stop striving to be your best! There isn't one day that I worked with Derek or spent time with him that he didn't want to do or be his best. He would arrive at warm-up early to do extra push-ups and sit-ups and would perform every night as if it were the last. Even recently when we went to Disneyland he made sure that we had the best time; there wasn't a ride that we didn't go on and there was always a certain way to approach a ride to get the maximum thrill out of it. Derek is a true friend and the ultimate professional and it was pleasure to have worked with him in *Footloose*. His direction, presence, charisma, and belief are the things that I love most about my buddy. Any dream big or small is a reality in his world, and since I've known him, it's been a reality in my world. He is a true gentleman who changes people's outlook on life for the better."

—GIOVANNI SPANO

12

REACHING FOR THE STARS

W HEN I FINISHED *Footloose* in the West End, I was utterly exhausted. I felt like I had crossed the finish line in a marathon, and all I wanted to do was go home, put my feet up, and veg. I also wanted to see my family—it had been nearly nine months. Idaho and my grandma and grandpa were my first stop, then Utah. I was enjoying catching up, filling them in about the show, when Julianne called me.

"Hey, D. I'm doing this tour called *Dancing with the Stars* and they need another boy dancer." This was the tour right after Season 3, the first time they had ever done a tour following the season. Cheryl Burke and Drew Lachey were going to do their whole "Ride a Cowboy" freestyle, and the two Joeys—McIntyre and Lawrence—along with Lisa Rinna and Harry Hamlin and Willa Ford—were all signed on as well. The tour would take them through thirty-eight venues, starting in San Diego and ending in Atlantic City.

"Well?" Julianne asked me. "What do you say?"

"Absolutely not." I had just killed myself for the past year and a half, and the last thing I wanted to do was to go dance on this tour.

Jules was persistent. "It's going to be all big arenas," she tried to convince me. "And five-star hotels. We're going to be traveling in rock star buses!"

I mulled it over. It did sound like a pretty sweet gig, but what really convinced me was my sister's honesty: "I don't want to go out on tour alone." She guilted me into it.

So off we went—Jules was just eighteen, but they had hired her as a company dancer. I was one of the background dancers, which for once in my life was just fine by me. Let me fade into the woodwork for a few months. I had had plenty of the spotlight doing *Footloose;* I was comfortable letting someone else shine. It was a blast—especially being with Julianne again—and when we wrapped, I headed back to England. Julianne was offered a spot as one of the pros on *Dancing with the Stars* Season 4. I wound up going to L.A. to do a guest spot with her: we did a groovy little number in week 6 to Joss Stone singing "Super Duper Love." We choreographed it in a few hours and it was the first time we really danced together.

After the show, one of the producers, Rob Wade, came up to me backstage. "Hey, Derek. Great job. You have any interest in joining us next season?"

I didn't even need a minute to think it over. "Nope," I replied. "Thanks, but it's not really what I want to do."

Back I went to England. Mark and I were traveling around with our band, Almost Amy, doing the grind. We were focused on the music, and we were very much a team. I didn't want to just go off to America without him. A few months passed and my phone rang again. We were still living with the Ballases, but in a new house. Corky and Shirley eventually divorced, and now we were living with just Shirley. The producers were still interested in me. Like Julianne, they seemed to have a hard time taking no for an answer.

I talked to Mark about it. It knew it would be a big transition—

relocating my life from London to America. While I was mulling it over, Mark got a call, too. He had sent in an audition tape and they were interested in him as well.

"Dude, if we're going to do this, then let's do it together," I told him. So that was it. We literally just packed our guitars and one suitcase apiece, and boarded a plane. I was aware that being on a live TV show in front of millions of people every week would likely change my life forever. I went into it very excited but also nervous. I knew a lot of the pros already through the ballroom circles, and I knew how good they were. I was coming in as a world youth champion—which is a big step below being a champion in the amateur or professional divisions. But on *DWTS*, the playing field was leveled. We were all starting from scratch, not knowing how good—or bad—our partners would be on that first day, and how much work we would need to do to shape them up. No matter how good we were, our partners were half of the equation.

I landed at LAX and went straight to Jennie Garth's house. I knew who she was from *Beverly Hills, 90210* (I used to watch it and had a crush on her), but I kind of still pictured her as Kelly, the blond, spoiled teenage princess—not a married mother of three. She greeted me with a baby on her hip. I don't think I was what she bargained for, either. I had recently lost some weight and I looked waif-thin and much younger than twenty-two. She gave me the once-over, and I could read her mind: "Who is this little boy who's supposed to teach me? I've been watching the show for a couple of seasons and I've never seen him before. They gave me a novice *and* a child?" But she was polite and shook my hand. "Well, you're just a cute little thing! You look like you're twelve!"

I was mortified. I laid it out for her. "Look, I've never danced with someone who is a beginner and I've never taught someone who didn't know how to dance. But I'm game if you are. I want to win this. Do you?"

She nodded, and we made a pact. We'd both give it our all. But

I was concerned right out of the gate that Jennie lacked confidence. "I'm worried I'm going to pass out on live television," she told me. I was still learning a lot at that point, too. I admitted I was really nervous as well—I was still finding my way. Thankfully, Jennie was graceful and a quick learner. But I knew I had a lot to prove. I was the new kid, so I never felt entitled. I had to earn my place there.

When it came time for the first live shows, Jennie was a basket case. "Nerves are good," I told her. "It shows that you care." It was a huge moment. During our second routine, the absolute worst thing that could happen did. I stepped on her dress and we both fell down—as Len put it—on our bums. As if that weren't embarrassing enough, they had to replay it in slow-mo while they interviewed us.

If Jennie was a wreck *before* that week, she was worse after it. But I tried to make her understand, this wasn't just about mastering the steps. She had to stop doubting herself. The fear was what was holding her back from achieving her true potential. "Listen, your worst nightmare happened. That's it. We got it out of the way. Shit, we did it—and guess what? Now we have an opportunity to come back next week and redeem ourselves and kick butt."

Which is exactly what we did. For week 3, we did a fierce tango. Jennie wore a slinky black sequin dress and I wore a black vest and tie, no jacket. The choreography was very complicated—lots of staccato moves, dips, twirls, and quick footwork. We had something to prove, so there was no playing it safe. Len called it "sharp and tangy like a pickle." Carrie Ann said we came back with a vengeance, and Bruno said we danced with fury. We got a 26 out of 30, a huge comeback from the week before. You fall down, and you get back up—that's the lesson I wanted Jennie to take away from this experience. Instead of allowing all that anger and angst to eat you up inside, channel it into the dance. Use that energy in a positive way instead of a negative one.

We danced for a total of nine weeks, straight through to the semifinals—and nabbed a perfect 10 from the judges along the way. It was either us or Hélio Castroneves and Julianne who were going home (cue the scary music). When they said our names, the audience gave us a standing ovation. We were both disappointed, not just that we hadn't won, but that the experience was all over. I knew I would miss Jennie. I came to think of her as a big sister, and I'd gotten used to her being in my life every day for the past few months. She is the most amazing, funny lady, and I wouldn't have wanted my first experience on *Dancing with the Stars* to be with anyone else. I was so proud of her transformation in those few months we worked together, and she changed me, too. I now knew I wanted to continue on *DWTS*. I wanted not just to take home that Mirror Ball trophy (that season it went to Julianne and Hélio, so at least it was a Hough that won), but to make a difference in someone's life.

Each and every one of my partners is different, but my approach is the same. At the beginning of the season, it's my job to make them as comfortable as possible. I have to break the ice and get them to trust me. I dance a little bit and I have them dance. I hold their hands and we make a physical connection. I let them feel the resistance of being with a partner, the push-pull. Sometimes I act goofy and joke around so they don't take it too seriously. There's usually a lot of embarrassment or even cursing: "Shit! Why can't I get this right?" I get it; I understand when you have high standards for yourself. It's hard to suck at anything, even something so alien and brand new. Nicole Scherzinger told me right off the bat that she was a perfectionist and a workaholic. "You have to allow yourself to *not* be good," I told her. "Just have fun with it. When you do, the energy shifts and you figure it out."

The first couple of days I try to get a feel for my partner's capacity. Are they flexible? Do they have rhythm? Can they count to music? Can they maintain information? All these things come into play. Brooke Burke, for example, has flexibility and when she danced she looked beautiful—but she had a difficult time with counting. I had to be connected to her the whole time and lead her with the timing of the music.

Sometimes it's not even about the technical aspects of the dancing, it's about the mental challenge. When I first met Olympic gymnast Shawn Johnson, she was very disciplined, as any pro athlete should be. We were doing the All-Star season on *DWTS*, and she had won Season 8 with (who else?) Mark. She was the youngest competitor, which was a first for me, and had this sweetness and innocence to her. She was also tiny—I didn't need to break out the Cuban heels for this season. But Shawn was at a totally different place mentally and emotionally than she had been the first time she was on the show. In Season 8, she was coming off an Olympic gold win. This time, she was coming off—as she put it— "a failed comeback," knowing that what she was best in, she couldn't be best in anymore. She was retired from gymnastics, and she thought she was doing *DWTS* again to reconnect with her competitive drive and passion. She needed to win this, not just to pick up another Mirror Ball trophy, but to prove to herself she still had the edge. She told me that since she had retired she had no confidence or pride in herself anymore. This season was going to be her redemption.

Our partnership was all about breaking the rules, upping the ante, showing the judges something they'd never seen before. We put trampolines in our quick step and crazy, dangerous lifts in our mambo. For our trio dance we went super tribal and pulled in good ol' Mark as our third wheel. It was a real risk, because it wasn't a traditional samba, but I wanted to push the boundaries. Len thought it was "self-indulgent" and gave us a 7, but the audience went crazy. Which, in the end, is what we were going for. We wanted to bring something different, and we did. And Shawn said it best: "We live for the standing ovations. We do it for the fans."

My biggest challenge was helping her shed her inhibitions. As an athlete, she thought she always needed to be strong and stoic. But I needed her to connect with her emotions and show her vulnerable side, too. It wasn't easy; she admittedly keeps a lot bottled up inside. So I gave her sexy side a name: Rosita.

"I need to see Rosita right now," I told her as we struggled with the rumba. "What would she do? How would she dance it?" There was a lot of giggling and blushing, but I needed to coax a grown-up, sensual performance out of her.

Shawn was nervous. "My whole career is about *not* showing emotion. I'm not an actress. I'm not comfortable letting my guard down. I hide everything. When you're vulnerable, you open yourself up to fear and pain and weakness." But I told her it was okay to show that side of her. I knew it was there, and it was anything but weak.

"Look, everybody knows you as Shawn Johnson, unstoppable and indestructible, Little Miss Nerves of Steel," I told her. "But you have the freedom to let all the walls down. Choosing to let people see your vulnerability is true strength."

We danced to the theme from *Titanic* and it brought the audience—maybe even Bruno Tonioli—to tears. I couldn't have been more proud of Shawn. I really felt it was the first moment when she connected to this part of herself. "You brought it out of me," she told me while we were waiting for our scores. I knew it was something she'd never forget, and I felt so privileged to be the teacher who helped her take the next step on her journey.

In the end, it was down to us and Melissa Rycroft and Tony Dovolani, and they took it home. It really didn't matter to either of us. We were so proud of what we achieved. Shawn got her mojo back and then some. And I learned a lot about why I do what I do. One of the reasons I get results with my partners is I forge a connection with them. I try to understand where they're coming from and what makes them tick. Often, I see something in them that they don't see in themselves: a repressed fear, deeply instilled self-doubt, a stereotype that they have never been able to shatter. I teach them how to get in touch with their femininity, how to be a sexy, strong, powerful woman who isn't afraid to feel or show all her facets. In this day and age, women think they have to mask their femininity to get ahead. People perceive it as a weakness, but it's the opposite.

I find that while each partner might have needed some specific coaching, the real tests we faced were basically the same, season after season. We had to learn to move as a team. We had to master complex, carefully timed choreography. We had to face the hot lights and live action and the idea that millions of eyes were upon us. But beyond that, I needed to inspire and instill confidence in each person I coached and danced with. I needed to communicate with an open heart and empathetic, encouraging words. I had to critique usefully and praise strategically. I also needed to be my authentic self—exposing my personal vulnerabilities to win their trust. Ultimately, I had to make each of my partners embrace not just me, but also her own skill and power. Every partner I've danced with has it within them to kick ass and climb mountains. When you put yourself in a situation when you're vulnerable, that's when your power is revealed. And it's always there; it's part of your DNA. It's like a woman walking into a room looking for the diamond necklace and realizing it's around her neck. I'm not changing any of these ladies; I'm helping them rediscover themselves.

And truth be told, that was never my goal. I never walked into a studio thinking, I'm going to transform this person's life. I'm no therapist! I was just trying to put some damn routines together! But I realized after all these seasons that the dance is a metaphor for the journey. Every one of my partners has had a very different one. What they brought to the table was different; what they needed to overcome was different. But despite that, the same thing happens time and time again: the walls come tumbling down and they find their true selves. That I have anything at all to do with that is both thrilling and humbling. In the beginning, I thought I was just along for the ride—arm candy.

To touch a person's life, to help them find their footing, is a gift, and I'm thankful I get to do it season after season.

Deconstructing the Dance

Each style of dance really gets you in tune with a different part of yourself. I was never content to do just one style of dance. I may have started out as a Latin dancer, but I had more sides to me that I needed to tap into.

CHA-CHA

The cha-cha was one of the first ballroom dances I learned. I remember doing it in a group at Center Stage to the song "I Like It Like That." It's one of the dances where you learn to isolate your hips: straight legs, feet grounded to the floor, toe leads. It's very staccato, with short, clipped movements intertwined with bursts of fluidity. It's a fun dance to do—it's supposed to be lighthearted.

SAMBA

The samba is a traveling dance—meaning you can bend your knees and move around the floor. It came from Brazil, and as with all the rhythmic dances, you create a figure eight movement with your hips. The torso and hips have to be flexible. The samba allows you to be very dynamic, shifting between the slows and the quicks. I love shakin' it and going hard! It's a party dance and it gets the crowd charged up. If you get a good song and you've got a good beat, you can really bring the house down. It's one of the hardest ones to teach a beginner because even when you let go, you need to be in control.

RUMBA

The first time I did the rumba, I didn't like it. I thought it was slow and boring, and I wanted the fast, cool dances. I didn't get the story behind it. Some people think it's a sexual dance. For me it's more of a loving, romantic dance. The small moments are suggestive and sensual. It's almost like the ballet of the ballroom dances. It's a slow dance where all your technique comes into play. If you can nail the rumba, then you've got your groundwork and your base. The rumba all about the control of your body: the internal resistance. It almost feels like you're wringing out a towel. When I started learning all the details, I loved it. The rumba also gives you permission to get very intimate and physically close with your partner. It's definitely become one of my favorite dances to do—but then again, it depends on who I'm dancing with and my mood that day.

PASO DOBLE

I enjoy the dramatic, intense dances the most, and paso is my favorite. There's a side to me that's easygoing, for sure. But I also have another side that's very aggressive and passionate. I love to explore this side when I'm dancing, and paso lets it all come out. When you stamp your heels onto the floor, it's like putting the devil down! You have to tap into the animal inside you: the strong, fierce beast that wants to attack. When I first started doing it as a student, I was all about that attack. My teachers had to show me it wasn't all external. Making an angry face isn't how you convey the character of paso. It's much more internal, the small inner moments and the breath. You can show your strength internally without unleashing too much.

JIVE

The jive is a fun dance but is technically very difficult. It doesn't look that way, but it's about showcasing your speed. Dancers consider it a true test of stamina. Usually in competition, it's the last dance you do, and it shows your ability to push through the threshold of fatigue. It's one of those dances that works the crowd up; the music is infectious. There is a lot of technique involved. The kicks and flicks require strength and focus. If they're sloppy, the dance loses its shape and control.

FOX-TROT

When I was doing competitions,the fox-trot was my favorite
dance. How slick could I be? How effortless and smooth? It's
a dance with grace and style that used to be done to big band
music. It consists of long, continuous, flowing movements across
the floor. It's a romantic dance where you and your partner stay
very, very close. Jennifer Grey and I did a fox-trot in week 5—the
halfway point in the competition—and she was relieved to chill
out with a slower dance. The fox-trot has a very old-fashioned,
1950s feel to it, and we danced to "Love and Marriage."

TANGO

I love the intensity behind this dance, which hails from
Argentina. It requires fluid movements, a strong frame, and
staccato footwork. When I'm in character, it feels like a
volcano is swelling in my chest—but I'm not quite letting it
out. When I'm really getting into the moment, my eyes start to
water from the focus and intensity. The tango I did with Nicole
Scherzinger to "Pretty Woman" was a great example. The
dynamic, the lines, the shapes were (as Bruno said) "portrayed
to perfection."

ARGENTINE TANGO

This is a more free-form dance than ballroom tango. I hadn't
learned it or competed in it until my season with Lil' Kim. I had
to figure it out step-by-step. I love the intricate footwork, the
lifts, and the beautiful story and passion of the moves. Kellie
Pickler and I did a great one, partially in silhouette so you could
see every line. It earned raves from the judges. Len loved it;
Bruno called it sublime; Carrie Ann said it was perfection.

LEADING LESSONS
Criticism can be useful.

I've taken a beating from the *DWTS* judges on many occasions. Most of the time, because I'm always aware of the cameras in my face, I just suck it up and take it. Here's the thing: I realize that maybe they're seeing something I'm not. Sometimes you're too close to a situation, too connected to it, to be 100 percent honest with yourself. Or your ego gets in the way and won't let you improve, because that would mean changing course and admitting you were wrong. I tell my partners to listen carefully when Len, Carrie Ann, or Bruno has a constructive criticism for us. Yes, sometimes it boils down to taste and opinion (and I don't always agree), but often it's a valid point. They want us to succeed. The way I see it, you have lots of choices on how to handle it: the first is to lose your temper, get defensive, and spend the rest of the night beating yourself up about it. The second—a natural reaction for most people—is to mentally shut down when someone points out your flaws. Who wants to hear that? Let me just drown it out and ignore it. The third option is your best: keep your mind and your ears open. You can learn about your weaknesses and how you can improve them. A leader is never scared of criticism, but instead knows there is always room to grow and improve. So bring it on.

Fake it till you become it.

Before *DWTS*, I was not a choreographer; I was not a teacher. I was neither of those things and had never attempted them before. So the best I could do was fake it. I had to play the part of the pro for the cameras. I couldn't walk into the studio and confide in Jennie or Shawn or any of my partners, "Gee, I'm sorry. I have no idea what I'm doing." I had to take the lead and be strong. When I was dancing with Brooke Burke, they asked us to do the Lindy Hop. I had never done it before in my life. I went on YouTube and watched videos of how to do it. Then I printed out a floor plan of the steps and learned it right along with Brooke. Did I ever let her in on the fact that I was a novice here as well? No. I just projected confidence and assurance, and she picked up on that vibe and went along with it. We did a damn fine Lindy.

My first Argentine tango was with Lil' Kim, and again, I was completely learning it as I went along. Now it's become one of my favorite dances to do. Whenever people say to me, "You're such a great choreographer," or I look at my Emmy learning it in my apartment, I remind myself that I came into *DWTS* with no experience, no education in many of these dances, and certainly no clue how to teach anything to anybody. I simply committed to learning them and then taught them to my partners. I drew upon how I had been taught and what I thought my partners would respond to. I felt my way along, just as they did, till I became the teacher I wanted to be.

I threw myself into the effort without hesitation because I had no choice. There were only two options: I could go out there and throw my hands up and say, "Just kidding! I'm a phony," or get it done. I couldn't let myself or my partners down.

This was the stage I was given, and I always want to be the best at whatever I'm doing. I never wanted my partners to feel they couldn't rely on me. I had to go in there and make it happen. With that mentality, I found a way.

Be real.

In work as in life, when you commit to a partner, you need to be willing to be personally vulnerable if you expect them to do the same with you. Letting down your guard isn't easy; it means revealing who you really are, your authentic self. For me, it has been the only way to make my partners feel the trust that's necessary to help them open up to conquering their fears. And in becoming vulnerable with others, I've learned many things about myself. Asking for help or admitting you're lost or overwhelmed doesn't mean you're weak. It means you're strong enough to allow your true self to be seen. Opening up to someone is the ultimate act of courage and faith.

REFLECTING ON DEREK

"Derek helped me remember to carry myself with confidence. Even when I felt completely out of my comfort zone, he reminded me to not underestimate myself."

—JENNIE GARTH

13

PUSHING THROUGH THE PAIN

WHEN I LIVED with the Ballases, being sick was never really an option. I remember one time, when I first moved there, I was feeling under the weather. My head hurt, my nose was stuffed, and I had a scratchy throat. Shirley came into my bedroom to ask me if I was okay.

"No, not really," I groaned. "I'm sick."

She handed me a glass of water and patted me on the head: "Outta bed. Off to school. You're fine."

Shirley held herself to the same standards. She didn't allow herself to be sick. Growing up in the projects of Liverpool, she'd had this ingrained in her. If you got sick, then you couldn't make your money, and if you couldn't make your money, you couldn't make rent. But her grin-and-bear-it mentality was very different from how my family handled illness in Utah. As a little kid, I got sick all the time, and my mom doted on me. She was such a nurturer and a giver. I loved getting all that attention and a day off from school. If I said I was sick, she didn't doubt it. She coddled me and nursed me back to health.

England was the exact opposite. If I had the flu, Shirley would give me a throat lozenge and usher me off on the train to school. There was just no sympathy.

"If you can't go to school, then you can't go to rehearsals. And if you can't go to rehearsals, you can't do the competitions," she reminded me. And just like that, my body obeyed. I literally never got sick when I was there because I knew I had work to do.

But I still harbored my old hypochondriac ways—at least when it came to competition day. If I wasn't dancing very well, I would think that my back was out or my hip was hurting or my shoulder was off. I always had some ache or pain, and it became a running joke among my coaches: "Okay, Derek, what's wrong today?" Shirley actually carried a box of bandages, aspirin, antibiotics—an entire arsenal of cures for whatever might be ailing me. I gave myself all these excuses for why I wasn't at my best. That way, if I didn't win, I had an ailment to blame. It was my defense mechanism, a way of dealing with my nerves and buffering myself from any disappointment. But after being constantly teased by my coaches, I started to look at all the other competitors and how they handled pain. They all had injuries, but they never talked about them. They just got on with it. I thought about it: Maybe I should give the stoic thing a try? Maybe I should stop making excuses and own my performance? When I did stop complaining, my body healed itself a lot quicker. I learned that the more I focused attention on an ailment or injury, the longer it stayed around. I'm not saying to ignore your health problems—just don't dwell on them. Acknowledge there's a problem, deal with it, then move on.

Maria Menounos taught me an amazing lesson about enduring. It was during our first dance, the cha-cha. There's a move in the beginning where she goes over my leg and I twist her, then she goes into another dip. A week before the premiere, we were practicing that move, but when I twisted her, she landed on my knee and cracked two ribs. Another person might have said, "That's it, we're finished here," but not Maria. She had her ribs taped up and went right back to work. She even joked about it: "Obviously, Derek's knee is very hard and my ribs are very soft." I was worried about her, but she kept saying, "We are not talking about this! We are dancing. I am having the best time of my life and I need to power through." When she got home, she'd ice her ribs or soak in a bath of Epson salts. As if that weren't bad enough, our second dance was the quick step, a dance with lots of jumping around and bouncing on the feet. In the middle of rehearsing, Maria fractured both feet pretty badly—three toes on her left foot and two on her right. Every day she would have work with *Extra*, then go straight to the hospital to have injections and get her feet wrapped. I teased her, "Careful, Grandma!" but I was in utter awe of her dedication and work ethic. She never once complained, even when I saw the pain on her face. Her doctors advised her to stop dancing, and she wouldn't. The woman is a fighter, and she genuinely wanted to be there, to learn, and to do well. She wasn't going to let anything hold her back from it.

But sometimes you do have to sit one out in order to heal. For me, that's a worse agony than physical pain. I never want to let anyone down, and I hate when my body doesn't cooperate. But I experienced this during *DWTS: All-Stars* when I was dancing with Shawn Johnson. I woke up one morning in agony. I had been doing a lot of tricks and lifts with her, so my body was taking a beating. I could actually feel my bones rubbing together in my neck, and it scared me. The doctor ran some tests and ordered me to take a week off.

"I don't really do that," I told him. But he was pretty insistent. This was a bad enough injury that if I didn't rest up, it would get a lot worse. I could wind up completely immobilized. I later found out that I have bone spurs in my neck from my years of dancing and whipping my head around. When the bone calcifies and heals, it creates extra bone on top of the bone. It closes the gap, but there's a small opening for the nerves to get through. The excruciating pain I was feeling was the nerves rubbing against the bone.

So for once, I took the doctor's advice and sat the week out. I don't know what hurt worse—the pain in my neck, or the feeling that I was letting Shawn down. I didn't want her to pick up on that, so I tried to hide it and pretend it didn't bother me. Sometimes the pain isn't only physical, it's mental as well. In this case, I had to power through my disappointment and frustration to keep my partner going. I owed it to her; I owed to myself. Shawn told me she had never seen me look so heartbroken and frustrated. But I shook it off, just like the flu when I was a kid. Mark, her previous partner, stepped in, and I choreographed the routine so I could still be a part of it even if I couldn't dance it. Instead of focusing on the negative of having to take the week off, I focused on the positive: "You guys are going to do a fantastic job and I'll be back next week to finish what we started." I've always performed, so for me not to be on the stage was a weird sensation. But I still felt the adrenaline rush. In a way, choreographing was even more nerve-racking than dancing. There was no control: I had to send them off and hope for the best. In the end, Shawn and Mark didn't let me down: they got a perfect 30. And I learned that even though I was injured, I wasn't useless. I could still be creative and feel a genuine sense of fulfillment.

It's a fact that a dancer's career is not forever. Eventually, if you dance hard and you dance often, your body is going to rebel. I do dance hard and often, but I don't think about that. I know there may come a point where I won't be able to do what I do now. I know a lot of pros who retire in their thirties. I've seen it and wondered, What if . . . ? But I keep it way, way in the back of my mind. Instead, I look for ways to defy age and keep my body strong and limber. I learn as much as I can about nutrition and exercise and I keep moving forward. Life is truly a series of transitions, from one season to another, from one phase to another.

I'm glad I had this experience of being injured, because I could draw on it when I was partnered with Amber Riley in Season 17. The *Glee* star had a problem with her knees from day one of our dancing. "I have really weak ankles and bad knees," she told me the minute she walked into the studio. So we kept an eye on that, but as we were going on, I noticed that Amber's body posture was all slouched over. When she would walk, she was giving in to that pain in her knees. She hung her head down and rounded her shoulders—what I like to refer to as "defeatist pose." But I could see right off the bat that Amber could move. I believed in her potential.

"I don't want you to use the knees as a crutch," I explained to her. "It's not an excuse to be second best. Yeah, you need to take the pressure off them, and there are certain things you need to do to protect yourself and to prevent further injury. But you have to get your head in the game." Week 4's tango was one of our hardest dances. We went to the doctor and he recommended draining the fluid out of her knees. Amber couldn't even start dancing till the Friday before Monday night's live show. There were lots of tears and lots of frustration: "It hurts to even sit down," she told me. "I don't want to disappoint anybody." We tangoed to Kanye's "Love Lockdown" and it was scorching (and earned us three 9s from the judges, including my sis Julianne, who was one tough guest judge/critic).

The samba in week 6 scared the hell out of Amber because it was so fast and the moves were a lot more complicated. We were also at the halfway mark—time to up our game. "I'm your rock, your support, your barre—whatever you need me to be," I assured her. "Whenever things go wrong, you stay strong." We got two 10s from Carrie Ann and Bruno, and an 8 from Len (what can I say? He found it a "tad repetitive"). The next week's paso doble really kicked our butts: my back was killing me, and Amber's shoulders were aching from holding the paso stance. By week 9, she had to go to the hospital and learned that she had torn a tendon in her knee. Could anything else go wrong? But I took a deep breath and shifted gears: "We just want to make sure we can finish the experience and finish it right," I told her. I had to change my strategy and create intricate choreography that would also save her knees. I choreographed a jazz routine that she could do sitting behind a desk.

There were a couple of times Amber told me or texted me that she thought she might need to quit. The word *forfeit* kept coming up. I wouldn't let her, just like Shirley had refused to let me stay home in bed "sick." It had always been Amber's pattern in the past: get sick or get injured and pull out. I wasn't going to allow her to continue down that path although I understood where she was coming from. I realized part of her pain was emotional—I could see it in the way she carried herself. I drove her nuts about her posture. I had to convince her that just standing tall would give her a whole new outlook. When you stand tall, your testosterone levels go up and your stress levels go down. I was constantly barking at Amber to stand up straight and "lift it up." I know I pissed her off, but eventually, she did it naturally. And when she did, her whole face brightened and her moves became faster and more confident. She found the determination and the strength to push through it. She's a warrior. By week 10, she got her fire back, just in time for the finals. "Amber Riley's back in the house!" I told her.

When we hit the finale, it was all about her taking the lead. Six fierce pros, and she completely commanded that dance floor. Bruno said it best: "You're a true leading lady." When we won the Mirror Ball, she bawled: "I didn't know if I could do it, but you can do whatever you put your mind to!" Mission accomplished.

It's one thing to work with a stranger on overcoming her pain. It's another thing entirely when that person is your mom. A few months ago, my mother passed out and hit her head. We're not really sure why, but she wound up in the hospital for a few days while the doctors made sure it was nothing serious. She was okay, just very shaken up by it. A few weeks went by, and she came to stay with me at my place in L.A. I saw a change in her—and it worried me. She was taking a lot of naps and complaining about getting old (FYI, she's only fifty-six!). This wasn't the woman I knew. My mom was always a ball of energy. She had had five kids and never slowed down for a second. Where was this coming from?

"Come on, you're not that old," I teased her. "Stop saying that to yourself."

"I'm tired," she sighed. "I need to rest."

I didn't want to aggravate her, especially after the scare she'd been through, but I wasn't buying it. I don't believe you reach a certain age where you just sit down and wait for yourself to decay. I thought what she needed was a little kick in the butt to get her back up and running. So I cranked up the music—"#thatPOWER" by Will.i.am—as loud as I could and dragged her up to dance with me. We were jumping up and down and twirling around, acting like idiots nonstop for ten minutes. It reminded me of our early days at home in our family kitchen, grooving to the oldies station on the radio. When I turned off the music, she was smiling and breathing hard.

"Okay, you can take your nap now," I told her.

"What? Are you kidding me? Let's go do something. Let's go outside. Let's go for a walk. Let's go jog. I want to do anything but take a nap."

I smiled. "Isn't that interesting. One minute you want to take a nap, and the next you don't want to stop moving?"

I sat her down and we had a heart-to-heart. "Mom, you're always trying to be this supermom," I told her. "But you also need to be Marianne. You don't have to do everything for everyone. You're a person, too."

I went out and bought her this beige leather jacket with studs on the shoulders. She looked fifteen years younger in it, and she felt it. I took her out to a party at a club for iHeartRadio and she was up till 7 A.M., dancing like a maniac. My friends couldn't get over it: "Your mom is amazing! She's so full of life!" That's the mom I knew. I simply had to reintroduce her to that self she'd forgotten. She was married at nineteen, so she lost out on a lot of her carefree, young years. Time to make up for it! As for the tired-old-lady bit? I was having none of that! You are who you think you are, and in my mother's case, it's definitely hot stuff.

GET MOVING

People are often scared of the word *exercise*. We associate the word with pain, and we think of it as a chore. (And it can be—who likes going to the gym at 6 A.M.?) If that's how you're thinking, then you need to change your psychology. I don't think of my body in terms of exercise; I think in terms of *movement*. Look at the actual word—I see it as "meant to move." As human beings, going back to the beginning of civilization, we've had to move to survive. We had to throw spears to hunt, we had to prepare land to plant seeds, we had to gather firewood. Our bodies are hardwired to move. Not even TiVo can rewire those thousands of years of DNA. This isn't a new idea, but it's easy to forget: your body is connected to your mind and spirit.

People say, "I'm miserable because I'm overweight" or "I'm overweight because I'm miserable," but these two go hand in hand. I know when I drink to excess or put poisons in my body, the next day I'm not going to feel happy or inspired. The body is the vehicle that can help you reach your dreams. Keeping it moving, strong, and healthy paves the way to overall well-being. You can't say you love yourself when you abuse yourself physically, and by not using your body, you're abusing it.

But here's the first piece of good news: you don't have to be in the gym to exercise. You just need to move—and keep moving. It can be anywhere, at any time. Sometimes I'll do push-ups during a commercial break while watching TV. Sometimes I take a short walk, even around the block with my dog, just to break up my day. Your body wants to move; your body was created to move. You have to feed that. When you're feeling miserable, your body is telling you to get on your feet. Moving makes you feel good. It helps you slay the demon of procrastination that lurks in the shadow of every human being. Most of us sleepwalk through life because we're waiting for the perfect time, the perfect place, and the perfect opportunity to improve ourselves. Stop waiting. Start moving and keep moving.

Find small pockets of time.
I like to set aside five minutes in the morning to squeeze in some push-ups and crunches. Just starting the morning like that changes my whole day. If you can find at least five minutes to do something that helps your body, you will already start feeling stronger. It will get your metabolism in gear, and that will benefit you all day. If you're too busy, get creative by doing something active during your lunch break, taking the stairs, or lifting hand weights while you watch TV at night. Start living by this rule: a little of anything is better than nothing.

Keep in mind the rewards ahead.
Workouts provide awesome internal rewards; after a long dance practice or gym workout I always have more energy and a clearer mind, and I'm able to focus on things I need to get done. But we all know it's hard to remember that great feeling when you're headed off to the gym, dreading the work ahead. Conjuring that ecstatic state of mind you know you'll find later can be a tremendous motivator. If you prefer external rewards, motivate yourself with baby steps every day to hit a bigger long-term goal—one with a luxurious reward as your prize. Once you've reached it, allow yourself to follow through with whatever reward it was that motivated you, whether it's a great glass of wine or a Sunday movie marathon.

Make exercising fun.

The same old routine at the gym can be a drag. It's good to mix it up. In addition to dancing I also enjoy hiking and swimming. And when you work out, do it someplace you find inspiring: a hike that brings you to a gorgeous view or a workout in the sand with the surf in your sight, even a small grassy spot in your backyard or a serene, uncluttered corner of your apartment. Recreational team sports also add variety to the mix: they put the focus on the fun of the game rather than the pain of the effort.

Cheat (sometimes).

Eating healthily is a part of my lifestyle, but I'm no superhuman. My Kryptonite is at the movie theater. I can't go to the movies unless I have popcorn (with butter and salt, of course), and I'll also get nachos with extra cheese and jalapeños, then some M&Ms, water, and a root beer if I really want to get crazy. It's okay to cheat . . . provided you do it only occasionally. If you *never* allow yourself to cheat, you put too much pressure on yourself and doom yourself to failure. Work hard and practice hard, but it's okay to cut yourself a break now and then.

How to stick with it.

Inertia is a real thing. Momentum will build. When you do something often enough it becomes a ritual, like going to church or brushing your teeth. You will eventually recondition your body to *crave* working out and eating the right foods. The circuitry can be rewired. There's the trigger, the process, and the reward. The key is to get it to the point where it's such a habit, you want to do it. Let's take a real-life example that all of us have faced: we haven't been to the gym in a while, we feel sluggish, and we don't want to go. The idea of lacing up the sneakers and hitting the gym feels like torture. The trick is to remind yourself that at the end of that workout, your mind will feel actually feel *pleasure*. It feels good. Sometimes we get brainwashed into thinking that *Gym*

= *Pain*, *Candy* = *Pleasure* when really it's the opposite: without fail, our bodies feel better after they've been in motion.

Fuel your body.
Think about your environment as an ecosystem. If there's pollution, you'll feel the toxic side effects; if you're in the fresh air of the mountains, you'll feel alive. You'd be surprised at how many of the foods that we eat actually *sap* our body of fuel. Just look at three quick examples: soda, potato chips, and hamburgers. I'm not a hard-liner who says that you should *never* consume these things, but this kind of steady diet will make it harder for your body to help you. Instead, look at the foods that are going to *give* you energy. Choose food that's water soluble and easier for your body to break down, which gives you maximum nutrition with minimal effort. Look at a cucumber: it's practically water and it takes no energy to consume, but it's packed with nutrients. Green for me is the key.

We overeat and undernourish ourselves way too much. When you eat bad food, your body will feel bad and then *you* will feel bad. It's all connected. I drink green juice every day and eat huge salads. I am also a big believer in lean protein to feed and fuel the muscles—I might even have a chicken breast for breakfast.

Growing up, because I danced every single day, I would basically eat anything I wanted and I wouldn't gain any weight. I would eat anything and everything trying to put on a few pounds, but it never worked—and my skin was terrible as a result of it. We'd blame it on the sweat from the dancing, but I never connected it to what I ate. As I got older, I started to educate myself more about food. I learned that I need to alkalize my body. It's never about how I look. Instead, I go by how I feel. I notice immediately how good, clean food boosts my energy while junk makes me feel lethargic. I'm also a huge believer in hydrating. Forget about eight glasses of water a day; I drink eight glasses before noon!

AN ALKALINE DIET

The pH level measures how acid or alkaline something is. Your blood is slightly alkaline, with a pH between 7.35 and 7.45, and your stomach is very acidic, with a pH of 3.5 or below, so it can break down food. Most of the foods we eat release either an acid or an alkaline base into the blood. Acidified body cells become weak, which can lead to unhealthy conditions and diseases. They are robbed of the oxygen and energy needed to support a strong and healthy immune system.

I incorporate alkaline foods into my diet every day, and I feel like my energy is soaring. Food literally acts like a battery for the body. Every living thing on this planet is made up of energy, and this includes your food. This energy can be measured in megahertz. Chocolate cake only provides 1 to 3 MHz of energy, while raw almonds have 40 to 50 MHz and green vegetables have 70 to 90 MHz. So if you need 70 MHz of energy on a daily basis to function and you live off junk food and soda, you are creating an energy-deficit crisis in your body.

People say it's expensive to eat healthily. Here's how I see it: you're going to pay either way. Either you're going to pay now for the good foods and feel alive and have a clear mind. Or you'll save some money now and pay for medicine and hospital bills later. I used to make excuses: I'm getting older, that's why I feel so tired all the time. But now I know it doesn't have to be that way. You have to make the conscious decision to nourish your body. Value yourself enough to eat well.

HIGH-ALKALINE FOODS

Vegetables
Beets, Broccoli, Cauliflower, Celery, Cucumbers, Kale, Lettuce, Mushrooms, Onions, Peas, Peppers, Pumpkin, Spinach, Sprouts, Wheatgrass

Fruits
Apples, Apricots, Avocados, Bananas, Blueberries, Cantaloupe, Cherries (sour), Grapes, Melon, Lemon, Oranges, Peaches, Pears, Pineapple, Raspberries, Strawberries, Watermelon

Protein
Almonds, Chestnuts, Whey Protein Powder, Tofu

Spices
Cinnamon, Curry, Ginger, Mustard, Sea Salt

LEADING LESSONS
Excuses hold you back.

Excuses they keep you from doing what needs to be done and from living your truth. When I was making all those lame excuses for why my performance was going to suck, I was refusing to own it. And when you don't commit wholeheartedly to a situation, you're always somewhere floating in the middle, never really operating at your full potential. We tend to make excuses when things don't go according to our original plans. Or we blame something or someone else for our mistakes. You can also make excuses for the things you don't do— why you haven't left a job you hate, followed your dream, or taken a risk. In the end, all those excuses add up to the same thing: a smoke

screen. When you make an excuse, you're rejecting the truth and trying to buffer yourself from the consequences of your actions. Leaders own what they do. This was something I had to learn through
experience. I saw how pawning off responsibility (like blaming a bad
back for a bad performance) was not helping me improve or grow.
People who constantly make excuses are often afraid they're not good
enough or can't live up to others' expectations. Maybe in the beginning it makes you feel better: "If I just explain it this way, I won't
look so bad." But the end result is always self-defeating. Excuses will
always get in the way of a responsible life.

Everyone has an inner warrior.

It's a silent voice—not a nagging in your head, but a warm, strong,
gut feeling of perusing and persevering. It comes in the moments
of stillness when you switch off your mind and let your instincts
take over. In Amber's case, her head was telling her that she couldn't
win *DWTS* with a wrecked knee. It made sense to her intellectually,
but her passion overrode her brain. It led her to defy the odds, and
prove—especially to herself and me—that she was fierce and fearless.
Her win inspired me, and it inspired millions of people who watched
her claim that Mirror Ball trophy. It's simply a question of unleashing
that warrior. If you can control your mind, you can control your life.
So in moments when you're feeling helpless, hopeless, overwhelmed
(you fill in the blank here!), that's when you have to let the warrior
out. Inside each of us is an abundant reserve of strength, determination, and courage. All you have to do is let it loose.

Ask the right questions.

Julianne and I were recently at our first rehearsal for a new dance
tour we're putting together. The first part of the morning went

great—we were having a blast, and we hadn't danced together in years so it felt amazing to be working off each other. We were excited, just ripping through stuff. We sat down for lunch and I had an idea for a lift. We decided to try it. Jules was in sneakers, and I flipped her around and her foot stuck. I heard a pop and saw her face. Pain rippled across it. We both knew it was bad but resisted the urge to panic. Her first question was, "How can we get this fixed fast?" Not "Why me?" or "Why did this have to happen today?" There was no self-pity or "Woe is me." The right questions put you in a positive place to deal and heal. Pain happens, but suffering is a choice. After Julianne asked me that, we got on the phone with our list of people who had great doctors and made the calls. She had X-rays and MRIs, and she's now in a boot to treat a torn tendon. But it's getting better every day thanks to laser and ultrasound treatments. Here's the thing: powerful people never throw pity parties for themselves. You will never hear my little sister moaning, "Why me?" when something goes wrong.

REFLECTING ON DEREK

"Thanks to Derek, I learned that I am stronger than I thought I was. Derek was a great teacher for me, because he made sure that whatever I did looked good on my body and felt natural. Instead of completely taking out a move I felt was too hard, he found a creative way to adjust it. The jazz number was my breakthrough moment. I had a new fire after getting such bad scores. Derek showed me that dance is just another form of expression, and anyone can do it!"

—AMBER RILEY

14

STARING FEAR IN THE FACE

WHEN I WAS partnered in Season 13 with Ricki Lake, she came into the studio with amazing energy and excitement. But I noticed that she wore this khaki baseball hat low on her forehead, just covering her eyes. That body language told me that something was up. As I started teaching her, I told her, "You need to look in the mirror so you can see that you're out of alignment."

Ricki took a deep breath. "I hate looking in the mirror," she admitted. I knew a little bit of her history—she'd lost more than a hundred pounds since she was the star of *Hairspray*, and she wanted to tone up now after having her second child. "These," she said, pointing to the backs of her arms. "We need to get rid of these right away."

She spent a lot of the first lesson apologizing for "not being Nicole Scherzinger." No matter how much I told her that it didn't matter if she had a Pussycat Dolls body and that she should be proud of who she was, it didn't seem to sink in.

"Check your posture in the mirror," I instructed her. Once again, the hat got pulled down as low as it would go, and all she could manage was a quick glance. "Ugh, my hips look huge!" she groaned and looked away.

Lucky for us both, I knew this fear of the mirror firsthand. As a teenager, I had terrible acne—huge boils on my face—and I avoided mirrors like the plague. But in dance, you need the mirror to help make corrections—in that respect, it's your best friend. I had learned that, and Ricki needed to, also. The studio was wall-to-wall mirrors from floor to ceiling, so there was no avoiding them. She had to get over this fear fast or we wouldn't be able to work, much less win.

We struck a few poses for the Viennese waltz and I told her, "Look! Look at that! See how beautiful you look?" She glanced in the mirror and her eyes lit up: "Is that me?" Over the next few weeks, the hat came off, her posture started to change, and an air of confidence took hold. By week 2, for our jive, she was gyrating around onstage in a skimpy sequin costume. We danced to "Hey Ya!" by Outkast and, as the song says, she shook it "like a Polaroid picture." It was an incredible transformation, both physical and mental. The confidence that she portrayed became genuine.

Ricki was a great reminder for me of how you should always tackle fear head-on. You have to put yourself in an environment or a situation where you have no choice but to overcome it—or it will overcome you. Growing up I was afraid of heights; if I looked down I got instantly queasy. So what did I decide to do a few years ago? Go skydiving with my sisters. I stood on the ground, waiting for my turn, watching them jump out of a small plane strapped to some dude's back. All I could see were these tiny blond dots floating in the air. Then one of the instructors (thankfully he was on his own and not tied to a Hough!) lost control of his chute. It got twisted and he began to spiral toward the ground. Everyone watching below gasped; he was plunging to his death. At the very last second, he pulled his auxiliary chute and glided down to safety.

After landing, he walked right over to me. "Phew, that was a close one. Okay, Derek, you're up next. You're comin' with me."

I felt my stomach leap into my throat. Are you serious? You're a dead man walking and you want me to go up with you? Then reason kicked in: What was the likelihood lightning would strike twice and his chute would fail again? And if it did, clearly the guy knew how to get out of trouble.

"Um, okay . . . I guess." I read the disclaimer and signed it. In a nutshell, it said, "If you die, we're not responsible." Thanks a lot.

The plane climbed to fourteen thousand feet and I stood on the edge of the open latch. The scary part is never the actual jump. It's the moment right before it, when you're counting down: "3, 2, 1 . . ." It's the anticipation of taking the plunge. That's the slap in the face. That's the moment your eyes are wide open and nothing else matters but the here and now. As you fall through the sky, the cold air slices into your skin and you can hear it rushing past you, louder than a train on its tracks. The world below looks so small, so insignificant, and then the chute opens and you feel this incredible gratitude and relief. Your fall slows, and you're floating effortlessly in the clouds. I think it's a taste of what heaven must be like.

So I did it. There is a tremendous rush in defying your fears—staring them down and daring them to mess with you. These days, if something scares me, that's reason enough for me to do it. I'm kind of a danger junkie. I love wakeboarding, skiing, scuba diving, jumping off cliffs. Many of my Instagrams show me jumping off stuff. My sisters are just as bad—Julianne especially. When we were kids, we'd go to Lake Powell, where there are these amazing red cliffs. I'd be peeking over the edge, trying to talk myself over the fear, and suddenly there would be this little body with blond hair flying through the air and breaking the water. My little sister always beat me to it and showed me up. People might call us reckless or careless, but I call it being alive. I understand now that nothing amazing is ever accomplished without fear. It's a sign that you're on the road to experiencing greatness.

But as a little boy, I didn't see it that way. I was terrified of the water. It wasn't that I couldn't swim—I did all the water sports you can think of. It's just that somewhere, in the back of my mind, was this fear that something lurking beneath the surface would suddenly drag me down. My uncle gets the credit for ingraining this fear in me. One time, on vacation at my grandparents' houseboat, all the cousins were in the lake at night swimming, and I fell asleep in the hammock. He thought it would be hilarious to toss me into the lake and give me a wake-up call. So he scooped me up and hurled me into the deepest part of the lake. When I hit the water it was pitch black and icy cold. I remember screaming because I had no idea where I was or what was going on. My only thought was to kick as hard as I could and reach the surface. I scrambled to the dock, terrified and coughing up water. It was a memory that stuck with me for a long, long time.

Fast-forward about twenty years: I was in Bora Bora on vacation. I was scuba diving, and thirty or so lemon sharks started hovering around me in the water. My first thought was, Wow, this is a lot more terrifying up close and personal than it is on Discovery Channel Shark Week. My next thought was, What do I do? I know the name *lemon shark* sounds sweet, but look it up. They are the ugliest, most terrifying sharks, and they get up to about ten feet long. That's big enough to take off your head in a single bite. I hadn't signed up for a shark encounter. In fact, they didn't tell us much about what to expect down there, and there was no training session. It was more like, "Are you certified? Okay, just jump in." After several minutes of being stalked by this pack of predators, I was overcome by a calmness. I remember feeling the sharks brush past my head and knock into my back. I couldn't keep my eye on all of them—they were everywhere—so I just let it be. They didn't bother me, and I didn't bother them. Instead, the thing

STARING FEAR IN THE FACE   145

that freaked me out on the dive was a harmless little suckerfish that decided to hang out in my face. Every time I turned around, he was there, stalking me.

Sometimes the anticipation of something is scarier than the actual happening. I remember being in a cab in New York City with a friend when I was young and competing. We were playing this game: I'd look out the window and he'd slap my thigh as hard as he could. The pain wasn't so bad, but the anticipation was unbearable. That's fear for me most of the time. I picture the worst-case scenario unfolding and I wait for that slap to come. Why do I do it? Maybe to protect myself. It's like when you cross your fingers to ward off a jinx. If I think of the worst that could happen, it won't happen. It's some warped insurance policy.

As I grow older, I realize that as adults, our fears are often self-inflicted. If you ask me what scares me today, it's something far less tangible than a hungry shark or a failed parachute. It's the idea that the best is already behind me. That I've peaked, plateaued, and I have nothing to look forward to, nothing to excite or challenge me. It's a variation on an old fear: that I've never been good enough, and I never will be. I know these fears aren't real—the things that scare us seldom are. They exist only in our undirected imagination, and they express things we love and cherish and can't bear to lose. But we also have to remind ourselves that fear is an emotion, and emotions can be controlled. Kellie Pickler admitted to me that she was her own worst enemy. She had a laundry list of things she was worried about, among them failing, falling, and just in general making a fool out of herself. I said, " 'Let's step back and name this nervous person—because she's not the real you. We'll call her Anxious Annie. You're Kellie and she's Annie.' " Once Kellie named Anxious Annie and called her out, she could separate from her. The next day—and I mean the very next day—Kellie had a true transformation. She identified and broke up with her own worst enemy and was way better for it. We all have insecurities. The trick is to stop asking why and instead ask, What can I do about it?

I remember as a kid seeing all these people riding a towering, loop-de-loop roller coaster that I was terrified to try. I just stood there, watching it race around the track at a million miles an hour. I was in an emotional tug-of-war: part of me wanted so badly to just jump on and try it, but the other part of me was paralyzed by fear of the unknown. What if it made me sick? What if I was so terrified, I embarrassed myself? What if the seat belt gave way and I plummeted to my death? The list went on and on and got gradually longer in my overactive imagination. People would get on and get off—unscathed and exhilarated. So I reasoned with myself, I'm sure all those people are scared, too. But they're not letting it keep them from going on the ride. Just like that, I got on. I screamed my head off, then went back for a second ride—this time, no hands.

LEADING LESSONS
Use your fears; don't let them direct or define you.

Fear sends your brain a message that it's time to make a decision— like when I decided I would ride that coaster. You can also decide to do nothing; you can stand watching the world zip by from the side-lines. I choose to see my fears as a green light. They mean go, not stop, and you're always in the driver's seat. Don't give fear any more power than it already has. As I said, I was often afraid of failure. But instead of letting the fear keep me from reaching my goals, I let it pro-pel me. In the movie *After Earth*, Will Smith's character states that fear is simply made up by our own imaginations. "Danger is real, but fear is a choice." Who knew Will was such a gifted philosopher? I agree 100 percent. Why is one person afraid of something and another other person isn't? We're all humans, but we've all had different experiences and therefore we have different associations. It's personal. The possibility of freedom exists wherever fear lies. When you realize that it's you who is creating this fear, the fear loses its ability to control you.

Break it down.

What are you really afraid of? Is it the water or is it not being able to breathe? Is it sitting in the dentist chair or not being in control of a situation? Analyze it and get to the place where you can see what's really haunting you and holding you back. I find that fears are not as big and powerful as we make them out to be. They're just made up of many thoughts that have woven together. Unravel them, pick them apart, tackle them one by one. It's like breaking down a wall, brick by brick.

The only thing certain in life is uncertainty.

When you're fearful of the unknown, what you're really unsure of is your ability to create your own life. Replace that fear with curiosity: What success or great outcome could come from this? What can I learn about myself that will help me reach my goals? Every one of my *DWTS* partners was worried about that first performance in front of the camera. I worried a few of them might even quit before they ever had a chance to perform. But once you hit that stage, it becomes crystal clear. The fear has nothing to do with the reality of that dance. It comes from not knowing what the experience will be like. Once you feel it and live it, that crippling fear vanishes. But you have to trust yourself: you have to take that first step.

REFLECTING ON DEREK

"I've been in this business for twenty-seven years now, and I hold Derek Hough right up there among the most talented people I have ever worked with or known. He is a visionary. I look back on my *DWTS* experience with him and I am so grateful and proud. I got to learn from the best, and he managed to get the best out of me."

—RICKI LAKE

15

NOBODY'S PERFECT

Even at my highest level of competing, I was never good enough. I was always finding the smallest details to fix. No one was harder on me (or my partners) than I was on myself. No matter how any of my coaches or fellow competitors tried to pat me on the back and tell me I did a good job, "good" was never good enough. The idea of perfection became an obsession—like a surfer trying to catch the perfect wave, I was always trying to find the perfect connection with my partner. I was in absolute terror on competition days—super intense and hypercritical. I was so on edge, you couldn't talk to me backstage. I remember once, I was furious with myself, and I blamed it on my shoes not fitting right. I took them off and hurled them across the floor, narrowly missing Shirley's head. Another time, I was so aggravated and upset with how the dance was going, I jolted my partner's arm during a paso doble and dislocated it. The pursuit of perfection was always my biggest downfall in all the competitions; it always crept in. I would basically start to self-destruct and want to stop and start all over. During practice that's acceptable because you have time to mess up, critique yourself, and improve. In a competition, there is no stopping. If it's a little messy, you have to carry on. That was so hard for me to do. It chipped away at my self-esteem. I would come off the floor and I'd be all upset and mad, and Shirley would have to talk me down off the ledge. "It looks a lot better than it feels," she'd tell me. That would make me feel better—for a moment. But I'd do the same thing again the next time.

Most of the time, I couldn't even articulate what I was striving for. It wasn't just frame or footwork—it was the steps you don't really see. The perfect balance of push and pull and tension. The weight of your body over your foot; the way your hips move through your center and move your partner simultaneously. The obsession was not what it looked like, but what it *felt* like. And because I was the one experiencing that feeling, I set the bar. No one could tell me otherwise.

When I went on *Dancing with the Stars*, I had to abandon that feeling. I couldn't expect a novice partner to understand the subtle details that it takes to create a dance. At first, it wasn't just frustrating; it drove me crazy. It was like going back to the basics of movement. I thought to myself, Man, I'm starting from scratch. Even if some of my partners had some dance training, this was a whole new experience. They had me to dance with now, and we had to connect and play off each other.

In the beginning, I struggled as much as they did. There were a lot of tantrums and water bottles being thrown across the floor (I'm talking about me, not them!). When I was choreographing, and it didn't come together right away, the dance routine felt unbalanced to me, which drove me absolutely insane. But eventually I came to an epiphany: Letting go of perfectionism doesn't mean lowering your standards. It means surrendering to the experience and the journey and allowing things to happen naturally. To be honest with you, it took me a couple of seasons to really feel comfortable enough to embrace being a little rough around the edges. I can see now that that's what it's all about, those human moments that the audience can relate to. If we were flawless from day 1, where would the excitement be? The journey of self-discovery is what the show is about—not nailing the steps.

Nicole Scherzinger was almost as big a perfectionist as I was. Not just with her dancing, but her hair, her costumes, the music. She told me stories of how she'd do take after take in a recording studio because she was never satisfied. That's how she is with everything in her life: she has very high standards. When it came to the week 10 finals, we had a rumba to "Lady in Red," and she was so focused on the technique, she was having a hard time getting the mood of the dance.

Carrie Ann came in to give her some advice. "You gotta live the dance," she told her. "Just let go of everything else and be in the moment. Let the edges soften." I thought Nicole did an amazing job, but the judges were looking for things to nitpick, and she was really upset. "I've done that dance better," she told me backstage.

"It's over, it's gone. It's only there now for us to learn from," I assured her. We had three more dances to do that night and I needed to get her head back in the game. "Think about it: You're driving and there's a giant windshield and a small rearview mirror. Ever wonder why it's so small? So you can only glance at it once in a while. If you stare and dwell on what's behind you, you're gonna crash." Our next dance, the jive, earned us a perfect 30, and in the end we took home the Mirror Ball. It was a great season and a great lesson for both of us. You can't get caught up in perfect. It's not about what the paddle says. If you immerse yourself every single day for three months in this journey, you're going to grow. You're going to learn stuff about yourself; you're going to overcome your obstacle—be it physical or emotional. That's what's important.

But I want to be 100 percent honest here: there are days when

I'm freaking out and I don't have the answers. I get frustrated, but I try and see it as a temporary situation and a separate entity from who I am. I step away from it. I've learned a ton about myself and how to manage myself and my expectations. There have been days when I've said to my partner, "I need you to help me today." I put them in the teacher role, and they wind up giving me the pep talk: "We can do this, Derek. We can do it." They're saying it, they're doing it, they're believing it.

Before *DWTS*, my work was instinctual and internal. It was something I could never put into words. But being a teacher forced me to dissect what I was doing and explain it. Some partners I could be really tough with and they'd respond to me. Others would shut down. If I got a little intense with Jennifer Grey, it was counterproductive, because she would block me out. But if I did this to Maria Menounos, she would get a fire in her belly and try harder. I have to learn to adjust myself to cater to each partner's needs and style of learning. If the look I get from her is deer in the headlights, I know I am on the wrong path. I have to find a way to make them understand. Great teachers strive to get through. My fulfillment comes when the lightbulb goes on and they experience that aha moment. They see not just what I want them to do, but what they're capable of.

LEADING LESSONS
Free yourself to have bad ideas.

Whenever I try to think of a brilliant new dance routine, it usually falls flat on its face. It's crushed by the weight of my own expectations for brilliance. It's much more fruitful to follow the advice of the songwriter who said, "When you write new songs, write for the trash can." When I start choreographing a new dance, I don't care how bad the idea is, and I allow myself to run with it. Challenge yourself to think of five awful, terrible, oh-my-God-this-stinks ideas. They get the juices flowing. And when you have those five, at the very least you have creative momentum and, more often than not, some of those ideas have legs. Think about the one thing that's original to you and no one else. What's your unique voice? Find that voice and shout with it.

Visualize the success, not the failure.

This part is tough for us perfectionists. We have a hard time ever seeing ourselves as winners; our heads tend to go to a place of "Nothing is going right." Don't get hung up on the minutiae. Say what you want, out loud, over and over again. Sound crazy? It works. Before I go onto the competition floor, sometimes I look in the mirror and say out loud, "I want you to do your very best, and I want you to be passionate and be in the moment." Giving myself those marching orders often reminds me to focus on the positive instead of getting lost in what might be wrong (but likely is just in my head).

Experience perfection often.

It's one thing to set the bar high, another entirely to set it so high you can never reach it. Keep it in a place where it's not impossible to achieve. You define what perfection is. Maybe today, it's running all your errands, and tomorrow it's noticing and appreciating a beautiful sunset. We're constantly told that no one is perfect; only God is perfect. But when we're born, we are perfect. I believe that person still exists in all of us. It's been clouded by experiences; it's been twisted and turned on its head, but it's still there. How will you define it and find it? I might think that dancing a technically sound routine—pointed toes, straight legs, sharp turns—is perfect. But someone else might look at that same routine and say that it's emotionally empty. Sometimes when you're not at your best is actually when you can be the closest to, and most authentic with, your partner.

An act of true empathy has great power.

The small act of accepting another's level of ability can be as valuable as coaching them to rise to yours. I used to have no patience for people who were depressed or upset; I didn't get why they couldn't simply snap out of it. I told friends and family, "Get over it." Now when there are people struggling, instead of just being dismissive, I try to relate on some level. That's life experience talking. I've been down and unable to shake it, so I understand better the challenge of mastering yourself and your emotions. When I'm dancing with my partners, they are completely vulnerable: not only are they being judged on their dancing and how they look in revealing costumes, but they are completely out of their comfort zone. Sometimes the best approach to build their confidence is to put myself in their shoes. What's going on inside their heads that's holding them back? Empathy is the power to see and understand what another person is feeling or experiencing. It's assuring them that they are not alone. It doesn't mean you have to agree with them, but you are acknowledging what they are going through. It takes time, focus, and effort—you have to listen. But it creates a place of honest communication and feedback where there was none before. I find when I empathize with my partners, the walls between us come tumbling down.

REFLECTING ON DEREK

"Derek made me believe I could do things I thought weren't possible. I had no experience in ballroom dancing and it's so technical, so at first glance the entire experience was overwhelming. But Derek is just such a great teacher. Instead of looking at the big picture and saying, "Wow, that's impossible, I can't do that," he took everything and pieced it together slowly and taught it to me like a puzzle. I focused so intently on getting every piece of that puzzle right. So after all of the hard work, when you pulled out to see the big picture, it was like a little masterpiece. Because he believed that I could do it, it made me believe I could do it. So we were like, "Let's just hold hands, close our eyes, and just jump off the cliff."

The most difficult thing he taught me was how to let go. I'm such a perfectionist. My head gets in the way a lot of the time because everything has to be a certain way and perfect. After twelve-hour days for two and a half months, after all the blood, sweat, and tears, he broke through and just taught me how to let go.

What's so special about Derek is that he doesn't ask the question Why? he asks, Why not? Creatively, Derek has no walls. He pushes the limits, pushes the boundaries. From one artist to another, he was so wonderful to work with. He was always open to new ideas and new possibilities, and not only as a teacher and partner. I learned and continue to learn about how to really cherish each moment in life and how to love and accept myself. Derek sees the beauty and the possibility in everything. He is magic and I love him, and the best gift is I won a lifelong friend from that whole experience."

—NICOLE SCHERZINGER

16

LIFE IS WHAT YOU MAKE IT

M Y LATEST *DWTS* dance partner has been a revelation. If you saw any of her performances on the show—or followed her amazing career as a snowboarder—you understand what I mean. Amy Purdy is one of the most courageous, dynamic, unstoppable people I have ever met. I truly run out of adjectives when I try to convey how amazing she is. At the age of nineteen, she lost both of her legs to bacterial meningitis. Her body went into septic shock, and she had a less than 2 percent chance of survival. Her legs had to be amputated below the knee and her spleen removed, and she lost the hearing in her left ear. Two years later, she also needed a kidney transplant; her dad gave her one of his. She told me that within two hours of coming out of her coma, she made two decisions: first, that she was going to survive, and second, that she was going to snowboard. Crazy? Maybe, but it was that drive that saved her life. Seven months after she got her prosthetics, she took up snowboarding and became a world champion. She turned her disability into her ability. When people said it couldn't be done, she proved them wrong.

Truthfully, Amy was exactly what I needed going into Season 18. After winning two seasons back to back and five Mirror Balls total, I wondered, What else is there for me? I couldn't imagine what more I could get out of this experience. I love to teach my partners, but I also need to feel like I'm growing and learning in the process as well. Then I met Amy, and she put it all into perspective. She gave my work a new significance, a new depth. She reaffirmed for me all the rules I've always tried to live by: Create your own life. Blast through the boundaries. Defy the odds. During one of our first press interviews, I casually told a reporter that my new dance partner was a double amputee. Amy took me aside later and quietly corrected me: "I don't usually say that. 'Amputee' implies that I've lost something. I say I have two prosthetic legs. That implies that I've gained something." The subtle change in language made her feel so empowered. I knew she was going to teach me a lot of other important lessons.

Our first time dancing together, I was really a spectator, staring at her prosthetic legs and trying to understand what it must feel like to walk on them. For me, the teaching always starts by aligning myself with what my partner is experiencing. In this case, her experience was nearly impossible for me to imagine. We had a lot of technical obstacles to overcome. This was new for both of us. I was nervous about throwing her around the floor because I knew she had the Sochi 2014 Paralympic Winter Games coming up. But she insisted I bring it and never hold back with her. The woman is fearless, and I love watching her face light up when she nails something. Yes, there are moments of frustration. Every dancer who is new to the ballroom feels it. In Amy's case, she had trouble memorizing the routine. So I tried to make it something she could relate to.

"You know how you memorize your course down the mountain— all the nooks and crannies, dips and turns?" I asked her. "Think of the dance the same way. You're going down a hill. Be in the moment and focus, then anticipate the next move coming up. If you make a mistake, it's behind you. Keep moving forward." Suddenly, she was able to do it. Something clicked. We quickly accomplished more than either of us imagined possible. I also got to travel with her to Sochi. It was a last-minute decision—we needed the rehearsal time before the start of the season. The *DWTS* crew was supposed to come with us and shoot rehearsal footage, but they never made it. I got my visa just fine, but because of everything happening in Ukraine, the officials got more strict about issuing visas, and the crew couldn't get any. I went over by myself and I had to film all of our rehearsals with a camera on a tripod. We also didn't have a rehearsal space over there. We rehearsed in the lobby of the hotel, with mirrors that only showed half our bodies. That made it virtually impossible to correct our bottom halves, but we made the most of it. Amy would train in the morning and then she'd travel down on the gondola to where I was at the Olympic Village to rehearse. She raced on Friday and won a bronze medal, then flew back to L.A. on Sunday for the show's premiere Monday. It was insane. For me, juggling the schedule wasn't hard because when we weren't rehearsing, I was just at the hotel or checking out the sights. But Amy was doing two things at once. Her coach and I made sure we coordinated our schedules and had a game plan. I assured him that I was being cautious about her well-being and making sure that we didn't push too hard. The thing with prosthetic legs is that your pressure points get really sore. Obviously, dancing and using muscles that she hadn't used before created new pressure points for her. I made it clear that I definitely knew that the first priority was the Paralympic Games. I had to keep an eye on her, too. She would want to continue to practice (because that's the person she is), but I would stop her and say, "No. I don't want to go any further. I don't want to jeopardize this competition for you." It's still remarkable to me—an Olympic athlete learning a cha-cha during the biggest week of her life.

From day 1, we were finding our way through this journey together. Different dances require different leg positions, and I discovered that when I let her legs click together, there were buttons on the inside of the prosthetics that released them. Amy shook her head. "That's not gonna work," she told me. But neither of us wanted to compromise the technique or the choreography. So we came up with a little safeguard. We put a bottle cap and duct tape around each of those buttons. That way when her legs smacked together, nothing unexpected happened. Still, you can plan and plan and take every precaution and things will still go wrong.

Minutes before we were supposed to go on for the week 2 swing number, I spotted Amy in the corner of the room, freaking out. There was panic in her eyes. "Derek," she whispered. "My foot's come loose! My foot's come loose!" Usually, it would be no big deal—she'd make an adjustment and tighten it up. But this time, she couldn't find her Allen wrench to screw it back on.

I ran around and grabbed one of the crew members. He had a Swiss Army knife in his pocket and that was the best we could do on short notice. I handed Amy the knife and she used it to screw on her foot good and tight. I thought we had dodged a bullet, but Amy didn't look convinced. Instead of being pumped to go out there, she was a nervous wreck. "I really want to do well. I want this to be a good one," she told me.

I knew I had to calm her down so she wouldn't sabotage herself. "Listen, every step you take is a success. We're all here, we're all rooting for you. Take the pressure off yourself. You standing here in front of this audience is a success." Her face relaxed and the tension in her body suddenly dissipated. We went out there and she did an amazing job. I was so proud of her. We hugged and high-fived each other as we took our place before the judges. No matter what they had to say, no matter what our score was (for the record: it was a 24 out of 30!), we won.

This past season was a lot more for me than just teaching a partner to dance. It felt like Amy and I were pioneers blazing a new trail. We never worried about the competition or compared ourselves to others. It was never really about the win. We were simply doing our own thing. There's no special dancing prosthetic. It doesn't exist because double amputees don't usually ballroom dance. At first, we used her walking-around legs that her prosthetics maker adjusted. Amy's done it before; she created her own snowboarding prosthetics because they're not really available in any market. We had to learn how to work with the prosthetics so they looked graceful and in control. In week 3, we got new legs. We found feet for swimming that have pointed toes. It opened up a whole room of moves that we couldn't do with the other prosthetics, and in our contemporary dance, we were able to add lifts and flips and use her legs in ways we couldn't before. This dance was for Amy's father. She asked me how she could thank her father for saving her life—words could never say enough. I told her that by taking advantage of her new life and living it to the fullest she has been thanking him every day.

Regardless of your religion, I feel like the best way to show gratitude to those we love and to our creator is by living our lives with passion, purpose, and happiness. Bruno called the dance "miraculous to behold" and there wasn't a dry eye in the room.

Second place is amazing. Neither of us had any idea what would be possible going into this. We are so proud of everything we achieved and created. I loved our freestyle. When I heard the music, "Dare You" by Hardwell, I knew it had to depict Amy's journey. It's what our whole season has been about: daring to go for it. I wanted that last note we hit to be positive and a dare to everyone out there watching: take the chance and see what can happen. When I began to choreograph our number, I had this vision of her spinning in the air, ascending to the sky and transcending the dance. I asked a friend of mine if he could rig a rope and he said it was possible, but it would take two weeks. We had an hour! The spin looked effortless, but requires tremendous back strength. Amy had been having a lot of problems with back spasms in the previous weeks, so we were a bit worried about it at first. But when she went up there, she soared. She did it with one hand, which was just incredible.

I have never been calmer in my entire *Dancing with the Stars* life than I was in the finals. Usually I'm tensed up and hyperfocused on getting it all right. But when we were standing there, I had the most amazing sense of peace and joy. I knew that regardless of the result, I would be extremely happy, proud, and fulfilled. I have Amy to thank for that. She brought kids with disabilities to the show every week. On one of the last shows, we had a ten-year-old girl with prosthetic legs in the audience, and during the commercial breaks she got up and started dancing around. I thought, You know what? That's it. That's what this is about. Amy didn't have that person to look up to when she was going through this. She's become that role model. So, honestly, that is the greatest victory we could have achieved.

I have always said that I believe that people come into your life for a reason. In Amy Purdy's case, she couldn't have come into mine at a better time. She summed up everything that I want to be and practice. When people asked her, "Are you doing *Dancing with the Stars* to inspire people?" she had a great response. "No," she'd reply, "I'm doing this to inspire myself. But inspiration is contagious."

LEADING LESSONS
There is success in every step you take.

When you take pride in every accomplishment—no matter how small— you create momentum and it builds to bigger and better things. With Amy, everything we achieved on the dance floor was something new that neither of us has tackled before. I wanted to cheer after every performance because we had gone where no one else dared. During one of our rehearsals midseason, Amy broke down in tears. "I have ten things I have to think about and I don't feel like I'm in the dance," she said. The dance was her personal story of what she had been through in learning to walk again, and it was dedicated to her dad, so it meant a lot to her—so much, that she was beating herself up for not doing it perfectly. I stopped her; the rehearsal was deteriorating. She was focusing on all the things she needed to work on instead of celebrating all the things she'd achieved in the dance. She was forgetting all the beautiful parts and editing them out. All she could see were the flaws. "Before you say what you need to work on, let's finish the dance and tell me five things that felt good and effortless." When she did that, she put her mind and body in a positive state of being where she was able to fix things much better and quicker. I told her, "Put your hands up in a V shape like you just won the biggest victory of your life." We walked around the room like this, reveling in it. We put on the music, and she danced it perfectly. When we finished, she had tears rolling down her cheeks. "I got really emotional," she told me. I smiled: "That's perfection—not the way you move your body, but the way it made you feel."

The only disability you have is between your ears.

We all have our disabilities; we all have our little insecurities—some are just more visible than others. How do you handle yours? Do you let them hold you back? I've learned that our brains play many tricks on us. Fear and doubt are only in your mind and have as much power as you give them. When Amy was lying in a hospital bed, being pumped full of fluids and fighting to stay alive, a doctor asked her what she believed in. "I believe in love," she told him. "And I've got a lot more love to give." It's incredible to know someone who's been on the brink of death and come out on the other side. Amy doesn't want sympathy or pity or special treatment. Her legs are her legs—she doesn't see them as a disability. It's not about what you have or don't have—it's what you give and you share with others. The more you put into something, the more fulfillment you get back in return.

REFLECTING ON DEREK

"Derek is connected to something so much bigger than himself—universal energy and light. His purpose is to be here and inspire the world through movement. We're very like-minded and spiritual, and we have great conversations. He's wise beyond his years. Here I am, a motivational speaker, and I sit on the floor utterly mesmerized by the words coming out of his mouth! Week after week, we are just experiencing things together without any end goal. We are in our world, seeing what comes out and keeping it organic.

Derek has also brought out this real femininity in me. I love dressing up and getting my hair and makeup done even though I'm a total tomboy/snowboarder. Working so closely with him, I've found this part of myself that I've never been in touch with and it's transferring into my day-to-day life. When we worked on our contemporary dance telling my personal story, we cried the whole week together. We knew we were on the right path if it made us cry. It was such a deeply moving dance for us. Right before you go on, there are always nerves, but there was also an emotional heaviness to what we were doing. Derek intuitively knew I was getting overwhelmed. He took me aside backstage and reminded me that the whole dance was about gratitude. He put his hand on my hand, then put my hand over my heart. He calls it 'stacking.' You stack all the things you are grateful for. He told me, 'You just won a bronze medal. Your family is here. You are so lucky to be alive and be here tonight.' We took the moment to breathe together and use the emotion I was feeling for strength and power. Whenever he does this, it fills my heart with such a positive light, I want to go out and share it. Working with Derek is an experience I will never forget. When I met him, I thought, 'This is so meant to be.' We were meant to come together to confirm things in ourselves. He is the embodiment of all the principles that I try to live by. The ancient Greeks used the word *genius* to describe being connected to an energy that flows. Derek is so connected with his genius, and I am so honored to have gotten to experience it firsthand."

—AMY PURDY

17

NEXT STEPS

THIS IS THE part of the book where the author usually sums it all up in a conclusion chapter and announces, "I did it!" I suppose I could have titled it "The Finale," but that's just not me. I don't think you ever reach a point in life (or in writing!) where you get to say that. It ain't over till it's over. I want to be an eternal student, always pushing myself to learn more, fear less, fight harder.

What lies in the future? Truthfully, I don't know. For some people, that's a scary thought. They like their life mapped out and scheduled down to the second. Not me. Not anymore. I take comfort in knowing not everything is definite. There's where you find the excitement, in the unknown, uncharted, spaces. If I take the lead in my life, I expect that things will keep changing, progressing, moving. That's the joy for me. Where will I go next? What doors will open? What doors will close? All I can tell you is that I will be performing and connecting with people—be it through dance, movies, music, or speaking. I want to inspire and create. I love the phrase "I'm created to create." That's what I feel like, and that's what makes me the happiest. I'm building a house right now—my own extreme home makeover. I love the process of tearing something down and rebuilding it, creating something from nothing and bringing my artistic vision to it. I will always be someone who likes getting his hands dirty.

But the blueprint of my life has completely changed from the time I was a little boy dreaming about fame. It's broadened and widened. I want variety in my life; I like my days filled with new and different things. I love exploring the world, meeting new people, learning new crafts and art. It's why you might often read what I'm up to and scratch your head: "I didn't know Derek did that." I probably didn't before, but I do now.

I met Olympic ice dancing champs Meryl Davis and Charlie White through an agent we both knew, Yuki Saegusa, and also through our mutual friend Kristi Yamaguchi, who won *DWTS* with Mark. Yuki reached out to me: "Meryl and Charlie, the reigning ice dancing world champions, would love for you to choreograph for their Olympic routine at Sochi 2014." I hesitated: "I'm not really sure about that. It's not something I really know how to do. I don't want to make a fool out of myself, and more than that, I don't want to give them a bad routine." Yuki understood. "Just think about it."

So I did. Whenever I am confronted with a "can't," I need to turn it into a "must." I agreed I'd meet with them and just see how it went—no promises. I was in the middle of the season with Kellie Pickler, and I had a lot on my plate. But when we got into the studio, I was immediately struck by their fire. They had tasted silver before; they wanted to go all the way. I knew that passion; I'd lived it. So we began working and we just blew through the routine. It had a *My Fair Lady* theme—a medley of "I Could Have Danced All Night" and "Get Me to the Church on Time" that combined elements of quick step plus lifts, spins, and tricks. Usually, I like to be part of the music choice, but this was their realm and I trusted them. I was excited; they were excited (and surprised by how fast I worked), and it came together very quickly. It was just flow-ing. They showed me a map of an ice rink: "We need to be moving in this direction, near the judges, then in this direction." When you cho-reograph for the ice, it's a whole different ballgame than the ballroom. I tried to imagine myself on the ice, picturing the movement and the momentum. We did this for a couple of days, and a month later, I went to Detroit, where they trained, and got to work with them on the ice. I am no Olympic skater, so it was quite a challenge for me. All three of us wore wireless headphones so we could hear the music, but no one else could (it needs to be a secret when you're at this level of competition). The most thrilling part of ice dancing is that you do so much more than you can on a wood floor. When I do a movement it stops; but when they do it on the ice, it keeps going. It's seamless.

Fast-forward several months later, and I was watching them on TV competing in the Olympics. They were amazing—the commen-tator dubbed them "power with grace," and I couldn't agree more. It was the first time in Olympic history that the United States won the gold medal in ice dancing, and that I could be a small part of that vic-tory is totally surreal.

Another opportunity presented itself this year from one more new-to-me genre. I was asked to choreograph a ballet for Misty Copeland to perform at the Youth America Grand Prix Gala at Lincoln Center. Growing up, I was never a fan of ballet. I hated going to class; I just wasn't into it. But once I started researching who Misty was and all the obstacles she has overcome in her career, I got excited. I realized how cool she is and how she is changing the face of ballet. I was also in a place in my life where I was tired of being safe. I really think sometimes I have two personalities that battle each other: the one that says, "You are so out of your league here," and the other that says, "Go on! You can kill it!" We danced to an original piece of music by the Taalbi Brothers, and I worked with District 78 to remix it. What I wanted to create was a group ensemble piece with Latin dancers behind us. The first day, when I got to rehearsal, Misty had already been there for about four hours, taking ballet classes with teenage girls. She has an amazing work ethic. I was immediately struck by what a beautiful woman she is, with an amazing physique that exudes pure strength. We started rehearsing, and immediately I was in love with her ability—it was beyond anything I've ever seen or danced with. She taught me a thing or two, and I'm so grateful for the experience. It was proof to me that when you push your boundaries, you grow by leaps and bounds.

I love helping people fulfill their dreams, but I also want to revive some of my old dreams as well. Dr. Dale E. Turner once wrote, "Dreams are renewable. No matter what our age or condition, there are still untapped possibilities within us and new beauty waiting to be born." As a kid, I had a lot of dreams. I wanted to be an explorer, an Oscar-winning leading man, a rock guitarist/singer. But I got into a groove and I began to let those dreams go and accept they weren't going to happen.

Now, I think I've reached a point where I want to quench the thirst of all my dreams. If they don't come to fruition in the exact way I envisioned them, that's okay. I at least want to pursue them. It's one of the reasons I signed on to do the movie *Make Your Move*. I've noticed that I'm drawn to storytelling—either through dancing, music, or acting, it's all about conveying a story. In this case, the character was a hoofer, a tap dancer from New Orleans. There's a lot of things I am, but tap dancer isn't one of them. I knew I would have to learn how—instant challenge. I also remembered how, when I was little, my dad used to tell me he wished I would learn to tap because it's one of his favorite things to watch. Again, I found myself in strange, uncharted territory. Everything I had done up to this point in my life was live: live TV, live stage, live competitions. Film is different. Whether you get it right or you get it wrong, you're still going to do it over and over again.

I was doing a dance number and I wasn't happy with how it was turning out. The old perfectionist in me came out; I was frustrated and angry with myself for messing it up.

The director came up to me and said, "Derek, calm down. We're going to do at least twelve takes of this to get the camera angles."

Oh.

I had to keep reminding myself of this: we're going to do it a gazillion more times, and then they're going to cut up and weave together the best pieces. I also had to get into a different frame of mind about how I wanted to convey this character. In live theater or on the ballroom floor, it's all about projecting and being big, but in film, less is more. I had to learn to dial it down, which goes against every fiber of my being. But seeing myself on the screen, I understand why that needed to happen. The smallest nuance is captured.

Another big new venture for me is my tour with my sister Julianne. It kicks off five days after the spring 2014 *DWTS* season wraps up. Julianne and I were both at a place in our lives where we felt like something was missing. We knew that doing a live show together would force us to grow and challenge our stamina, endurance, and creativity. It was daunting and terrifying, but all the good stuff in my life has started for me with complete terror. Once I convinced myself, convincing my sister was easy.

We thought at first we would do a live show in Las Vegas and the Venetian wanted us to put it on after Faith Hill and Tim McGraw checked out. But the more we pondered the idea, the more we realized that we didn't want people to come see us. We wanted to go see them. We wanted to go into their towns and cities and reach them. We weren't sure what the demand would be, but we were inspired. Everything seemed to fall into place after that decision was made. We know how important moving is in our lives, so the name of the tour became Move. It has a double meaning. Everything in the world is moving, but there's also the emotional side: what moves you? We talked a lot about how we could create a show where we have the audience interact with us. We wanted them to leave the theater feeling out of breath. We wanted the show to feel like a big party or a rock concert—no one sits this one out.

Starting up rehearsals was interesting. Julianne hadn't danced like this in four years and she was nervous. But it was like riding a bike. We picked up right where we left off. In our first rehearsals, she was going for it more than ever—she's such a daredevil. Everything I did, she wanted to do and then some. That old competitive side comes out. For me it felt like the first season of *DWTS*, because that was really the first time we danced together. People asked us a lot about who would be calling the shots and creating the routines. Honestly, it's been totally collaborative. We rarely disagree and we both land on similar things. If I say something isn't good enough, then she has a suggestion on how to fix it. I love watching her finding her voice again in that area of creativity. The confidence is back (it was back within the first hour of rehearsals!).

Jules and I have a lot of respect for each other. We happen to be brother and sister and have that chemistry and connection, but we both respect each other as performers and artists. We're proud of each other. Not to embarrass her (okay, I will), there have been times in my life where I'm down and she'll send me a text: "Listen, you're the most important man in my life besides Dad. I don't know anybody like you, you're the most incredible human being." That's really humbling coming from your sister. When we dance we don't really even talk to each other; we just kind of do it. She throws herself into movements and I'll catch her and hold her. We have that connection, that unspoken language when we dance. We haven't toured like this since that first *DWTS* tour when she convinced me to come along for the ride. There's no person I'd rather be on the road with than my sister. So we're on this adventure together.

When you do so many different things, the plus is, you're putting yourself out there. The minus is, you're putting yourself out there. People ask me all the time if I like being stopped on the street by fans, and if it's fun to be famous. I won't lie: it can be a very good thing. Case in point: winning my Emmy for Outstanding Choreography in 2013. After the ceremony, I went to the Governor's Ball to get the plaque put on the trophy. It's pretty cool: They already have your name engraved, but you get to watch them put it on the base. Then we went to the HBO party and the AMC party, where all the *Breaking Bad* people were. Aaron Paul and Dean Norris were hanging out there. I was walking around with my trophy in hand and I felt pretty awkward. "No man," Aaron told me. "Don't feel stupid. This is the night you walk around with this thing. Any other night, it would be kind of weird and sad. But this night, you hold it high!" It was a cool night. We danced full-out. Normally when I go out, I don't dance but I thought, Whatever, I'm going to dance my ass off and celebrate. Dean was a mad man on the dance floor. There was a moment when "We Are the Champions" came on and he took my Emmy and started fist-pumping with it. I know there are lots of pictures out there from the party, but they don't do it justice! It was so much fun. And Dean was throwing down moves! He can *dance*. It was Breakdancing Bad!

Beyond the partying, the moment had a great deal of meaning for me. I didn't just win the Emmy for myself; I won it for the show, and all the people who work so hard and all the years we've been doing it. I am truly a huge fan of all the other nominees, but it felt great to bring one home for *DWTS*.

If I'm ever tempted to let it get to my head, all I have to do is remember the first time I was recognized in public. I was with Jennie Garth, back in Season 3. She was way more famous than me (Derek Who?) and she was asked to the Eiffel Tower ceremony at the Paris Las Vegas hotel. They shut off half the strip and there were thousands of people outside the hotel lined up to see it. I was onstage supporting her, when I was suddenly hit with a wave of nausea. I knew instantly I had food poisoning from something I'd eaten earlier in the day. I knew if I didn't get off the stage at that moment, I was going to throw up—and that would be the story on the evening news, not Jennie's lighting!

I jumped off the stage and just wanted to get back to my room where I could vomit in peace. As I was racing through the hotel lobby, a few people stopped me. "Aren't you Derek Hough from *Dancing with the Stars*?" I was trying to be polite, but I just kept eyeing garbage cans in case I couldn't hold it in any longer.

"Yeah, thanks," I said. I signed a few autographs and tried to push my way to the elevators.

"Wait! Derek! Can I get you to sign this?" More people started coming at me. I swear, I had to hold my breath so I wouldn't hurl! When I finally got upstairs, I threw up thirty-two times. I was deathly ill. But somewhere, in that haze of hellish food poisoning, it hit me: This is pretty cool! People know who I am! But I've tried my hardest not to let that change me. I'm kind of a free spirit; what you see is what you get. Inside is still that crazy little boy who liked to bounce off his living room walls.

Which brings me to my very last leading lesson for you: Live now. Truthfully, it's something I struggle with every day. Being a choreographer, I need to constantly envision the future—what a routine might look like before it's ever danced. You see a blank dance floor; I see bodies moving across it in an intricately woven series of moves. I suppose this is a good thing for a guy who competes on *Dancing with the Stars*, but it's not such a good thing for my well-being. That "forward thinking" began to bleed into my everyday life as well, and for a long time, I would find myself in a constant state of worry about the future. I was anxious and relatively unhappy considering all my successes, and I didn't know why. The day would fly by and I wouldn't even remember what I did, because I was just going through the motions. Then it dawned on me: I wasn't in the moment.

It's good to have goals for the future and it's good to learn from the past, but life is happening *now*. You cannot let it rush by you unseized or unacknowledged. You have to make a real, conscious effort to be in the present and not let your thoughts drift to other places and times. Your mind is an instrument, a tool. It is there to be used for specific tasks, and when the task is completed, you lay it down.

This is a tough thing for me. I'm an overthinker. Many of us are. My mind gets racing a thousand miles a minute and I get anxious about my work, my career, or where I need to be in thirty minutes. Every day I need to shut down this machine and simply *be still*.

Be aware of your breathing, really feel your breath going in, going out. Be aware of the feeling of the cloth on your shirt. Be aware of the grip on the steering wheel. Tell yourself—out loud— that the only thing that truly exists right now is this exact moment, and enjoy it, swim in it. Someone once said that your mind is like a raging river that's full of debris, and when you're floating in this river, you reach out and try to grab the branches and rocks. But what if you could climb onto the bank and watch the river? Suddenly you're in a calm place.

Maybe it sounds like a cliché to say, "Stop and smell the roses," so I'll tell you this instead: "Stop and watch the sunset." Just the other night, driving home in L.A., I was struck by how beautiful the sky was—a dark blue canvas painted with strokes of bright orange and red. It was truly one of the most glorious sunsets I'd ever seen. I was stuck in traffic, worrying about one thing or another, and I just gazed out the window and drank it in. I let it fill my soul and inspire me. The world stopped revolving for just that split second, and my mind was still and calm.

And to think, I could have missed it.

REFLECTING ON DEREK

"While working with Derek, Meryl and I learned some really great steps and combinations of steps that we could use in our Olympic short dance. He sent us in a great direction for when we needed to figure out where we wanted to take the program. Beyond the amazing ballroom steps that we worked on with Derek, I think we learned a lot about how to show our love of dance through our movements by watching Derek. His zest for life really comes through when he dances, and that was something we wanted to capture as well. Derek helped us win the Olympic gold medal by helping to set us up with an Olympic gold medal–worthy short dance, and by being a great inspiration for how to show our passion through our movements."

—CHARLIE WHITE

ASK DEREK:
Q&A

P EOPLE ARE ALWAYS asking me questions. I get tons on Facebook and Twitter, and people even stop me on the street. The questions are not just about dance; I get everything from "How do I lose 50 pounds?" to "You're great at getting your partners to listen to you. How do I get my husband to do the same?" So when I put out the word that I was seeking questions for my book, I was flooded with tons of great ones. I couldn't possibly answer them all, but I did my best to give you a good assortment.

DANCING . . . .

Are there ever times when you feel like you don't love (or even like) dancing? If so, what do you do to regain your joy for it?

There are definitely times—not that I don't like dancing—but when I reach a point when I don't feel challenged by it. The steps are overly simple, or the music is boring, and I definitely get into a place of not enjoying it. These are the times when dancing feels more like a job than something I love. When that happens, I have to step away from it. If I'm getting tired of dancing or choreographing, I'll go to a concert and rock out, or jump on a wakeboard. I take myself as far away from it as I can. Then when I come back to it, it's like dancing for the first time.

Can you recommend a dance style for beginners with two left feet?

A good place to start is a cha-cha. It's got a very defined rhythm—you can't go wrong with it. But here's the thing: you're going to pick up the dances you enjoy quicker. So try lots of different styles and see what feels right to you. What kind of music do you like? Motivate yourself!

If you could dance with anyone on the planet—living or dead—who would you choose to do a duet with and why?

Honestly, I think it's evolved for me. When I was younger, Michael Jackson would have been the ultimate duet. He blew me away. Now, after seeing so many movies, I have to say I would like a trio: Fred Astaire on the drums, Gene Kelly on the taps, and me filling in the gaps.

What would you share with a dance student to help her get rid of self-doubt or performance anxiety?

Take the pressure off yourself. You're creating a story that hasn't even happened: you messing up or the audience laughing. Get rid of it. Envision enjoying it and the audience loving it. Create a different image and put yourself in a better place. Enjoy it. It sounds like a cliché to say, "Go out there and have fun," but it's true. Whenever you feel that anxiety, catch it, realize what you are doing, then rewrite the story. Think of three things you are grateful for in that moment and go out there and embrace the dance.

I want my grandparents to dance like they used to when they were young. They say they're too old. Any advice?

Hell, yeah! When I hear people tell me, "I'm too old to dance," I say you're never too old! I go to this salsa club in L.A. and I see seventy-, eighty-, and ninety-year-old people dancing their butts off. They are moving and loving it. I recently popped into my grandparents' place in Idaho for a visit. They're in their eighties, and my grandpa has had some serious health issues. He's had three quadruple bypasses. It was midnight, and they were in their pajamas. My grandma tells me, "Derek, every single morning we wake up and turn on this song and dance." Then she proceeds to demonstrate! She goes over and puts on a song and they start dancing. I've never seen them light up so much—they looked twenty years younger. Lesson learned? Your grandparents can and should dance. Even people who are in wheelchairs or confined to bed, can still dance and move. Remind them of that!

I see how dance transforms the bodies of the stars on the show. I need to lose weight—can it do the same for me? I'm so unmotivated!

Absolutely. Dancing you enjoy, so you forget that you're working out. We associate working out with work and with pain. But dancing is fun and you should go for it if it motivates you to move. All consistent movement helps your metabolism. But I'm not going to say don't change anything else in your life. You have to be consistent with how often you move, and you need to eat healthily. You can't dance in the morning and eat cheeseburgers and fries for lunch. What you see on *DWTS* is a combination of people dancing and changing their habits and their whole lives. In order to do the show, they need to be stronger and they need to be fueled. Your body is your machine; you've got to make sure it's well-oiled.

DANCING WITH THE STARS

How difficult was it during the first few seasons of *Dancing with the Stars* when you were competing against Mark and Julianne?

It wasn't hard for me because we competed against each other growing up. Those days, it was hard-core competition. This felt a little more like fun competition for us. But when Julianne beat us that first season, Mark and I both said, "Well, that feels weird!"

Is it difficult to separate the chemistry created on the dance floor and the real connection you may feel for your partner?

It is by nature an intimate situation when you're dancing with someone that closely. There have been times when a partner came into rehearsal and told me, "I dreamed about you last night." We both laugh about it and carry on. People think that you need real chemistry to pull off an emotional or a sensual dance, but that's not the case. If you have two people and you are each honest with yourselves, then you will create a connection on the dance floor.

Tell us something we don't know about what goes on backstage at *DWTS*! Any secrets? Anything we don't see on camera?

I don't want to divulge *all* our secrets, but here's a good one: there have been a few wardrobe malfunctions in the past, especially with ladies and parts of their anatomy popping out. Obviously being on national TV, we want to avoid these fashion emergencies, so the women wear these things called pasties. We have an official person, a woman, who's in charge of pasty checks. It's her job (I'm not kidding) to makes sure nothing is revealed when it isn't intended to be.

Is Len as grumpy as he seems? Does Carrie Ann always cry? Can you understand what Bruno says (I can't)? Do you get along with all the judges?

I knew Len back when I was a kid in London. Sometimes, he'll come up to me in the hallway after he's just blasted me onstage and say, "I loved it. That was bloody marvelous." So much for being tough! He's a great guy and I think he's brilliant at what he does. He has a great way with words. I admire all the judges. As for Carrie Ann, good for her for being so open. It makes me happy when I see her get emotional. Bruno's just crazy. Enough said. As long as he keeps his shirt on, I'm good.

Who has been your favorite guest judge so far on *DWTS* and why?

Cher. The first time she gave a score, she didn't say the number, she said her name. Carrie Ann says, "Seven;" Bruno says, "Seven," and she says, "Cher!" I just thought that was absolutely priceless and hilarious.

Have you ever had to change a dance last minute? Why?

Oh, yeah. That's what a choreographer's job is—to be very flexible. With my partners, there have been times when we would be too nervous of the step and I've had to edit it out right before the live show. Amber is a great example. There was a move where she was supposed to grab me and I did a backflip. In rehearsal, I knocked her in the head. It made her too nervous, so we took it out right before we went onstage to perform it. I'm always changing things last minute, and I base it on what's best for my partner and the dance. I used to be very set in my routines, but experience has taught me that you have to be able to change things at the drop of hat to get it done.

Do you hang out with the *DWTS* pros after the show? Are you guys friends?

We definitely all get along and support one another, out and about. We've known each other a long time. At the premiere of my movie, Val came to the after party. I finished all my press and I said, "Do you want to go watch the end of the movie?" I have a really tough time watching myself on screen so all I wanted to do was get out of the theater. Val could sense how uncomfortable I was and he knows how self-critical I am. He said to me, "Dude, you looked great up there. Are you gonna win an Oscar for it? No! But you're on the right track." I thought that was hilarious—nothing like a friend to put it all into perspective for you!

Is the Mirror Ball heavy? Where do you keep yours?

Yeah, they're pretty heavy—but not very durable. They break easily. I keep all of mine downstairs in my office tucked away on some shelves. I don't have them scattered around the house—that would be a little obnoxious. When the light hits them at the right time of day, it's like you're in Studio 54.

Do you design all the costumes for you and your partners? Has anyone ever not liked your fashion choices?

Mark Ballas is like, "I wanna be a wizard, I wanna be a ninja." He loves a good costume. Me? Put me in a T-shirt and jeans and I'm happy. But somehow I've become good friends with the wardrobe department in all my seasons on the show. I work really closely with them. They let me guide them. With Amy in her contemporary costume, it first felt too sexy. It was peach and I thought the color was a mistake; it made the prosthetic leg look orange. Last minute, I said, "Let's make a basic grey dress." I didn't want to see the costume—I wanted to see her. I actually sketched the costume on a piece of paper. I never thought

I'd be designing clothing! But getting the fit right and getting the fabric to do what it's supposed to do is part of my job.

How has your experience on *DWTS* changed you? For better or for worse?

Definitely for worse—no, I'm kidding! It's transformed me. I was very much self-concerned in my early career; it was all about me. But this show is not about you, it's about your partner and bringing the best out in them. I want them to shine. Taking another human being on a journey from no experience to something extraordinary in a short amount of time is a great gift. It taught me patience and compassion. It's been an incredible experience that I am so grateful for.

Who comes up with those crazy team names—and what has been your favorite?

The fans! I think my favorite has been "Menough Said" for Maria Menunos and me.

PARTERSHIPS

You have the gift of bringing out the absolute best in your partner, no matter who she is. Any tips for the rest of us? How can we learn to bring out the best in our own partners?

The first time I work with a partner, I'll put the music on and I'll watch them move in the mirror naturally. I will choreograph the dance, building on that natural ability. I don't force them into changing into something completely different than who they are. It's never "do what I do." So to answer your question, I say start by identifying something your partner does well—the great qualities he or she already has—and build on them. Don't try to force someone to be who they're not. Appreciate what makes them unique and special.

My boyfriend is not great at communicating. How can I encourage him to be more open?

When I go in the studio, I take on a role. I have to be someone who can communicate something so my partner can understand it perfectly. You have to be what you want from people. You have to start with your own honesty and openness to get it back in return.

LIFE IN GENERAL . . . .

What makes you so happy? You are always smiling. What is your key to being so happy?

Let's be clear—I'm not always happy. There are days I want to jump off a cliff. But saying that, even on my bad days, I make a conscious decision to be happy. You have to make that decision every day, many times a day. I want to be happy, so I am.

You have a lot of great motivational quotes, but is there one book that is your favorite? A saying that you always live by?

A book that really resonated with me was *The Power of Now* by Eckhart Tolle. I was living so much in the future and had such anxiety, and that book came along and those four words were life-changing. The sayings that motivate me change frequently; it's based on the timing. Right now I like "Follow less people on Twitter and lead more in life."

In the midst of all the success that you have encountered, how have you managed to remain so normal and genuine? How do you *not* let fame get to your head?

My family definitely keeps me grounded. Also, I don't consider myself famous. Nobody is any better than anybody else. We're all just human beings.

What's a song that inspires you no matter what is going on in your life?

Everyone has a song that hits them at an important time in their life. Maria Menounos said hers was Madonna's "Material Girl." I was like, "Really? Okay."

For me, that song is "Sweet Disposition" by The Temper Trap. I heard it at a time in my life when everything was becoming clear, and I'm anchored to it. Every time I hear it, I feel hopeful. It reminds me of dusk. It makes me feel happy to be alive.

If you couldn't dance, what would you do?

I love architecture—I think I'd be an architect. I'd be someone who creates something from nothing. That's what I do in my choreography as well.

Everyone makes mistakes—so what is your biggest one?

The biggest mistake I make all the time is starting to doubt myself. There have been a lot of moments of doubt, but in particular, it would be the time our record label dropped us. It made me question myself and my talent, and that doubt led me down certain roads until I didn't like who I became. I had been so sure and confident, and for a moment, I thought, Maybe, I'm not that guy.

I would love to hear about your experience dancing with Brilynn Rakes. You were crying at the end of the dance. She passed away suddenly a week after that spotlight segment aired. I know it was a highlight of her life and it appeared to touch you deeply.

It was pretty remarkable, and it's such a gift to be let into someone else's life in this way. This girl who has no sight decided she wants to be a ballerina—and who says that she can't be one? She knew her limitations and she defied them. It moved me a lot, and it chokes me up even now when I write about it. For the segment, *DWTS* interviewed her dad for an hour and a half and he said he was so proud of her and how much joy she brought into their lives. *DWTS* sent her family all that footage. Things truly do happen for a reason. Maybe doing this dance gave Brilynn the opportunity to hear her father say these things about her. Now that she's gone, he has that to hold on to.

Do you have a bucket list? And if so, what are some of the things on that list?

My bucket list is never-ending! I want to get my Indiana Jones hat on and travel the world. I want to take my mom to Paris and paint for a week, and my dad and I have always talked about hiking the Alps (I've got to get on that!). I want to try cave diving—kind of like scuba diving, but you go into these massive caves underwater with a flashlight. It would be terrifying, but incredible.

If you could pick one of the following three women for a dance partner, who would you choose and why: Lady Gaga, Michelle Obama, or Kate Middleton?

I'd like to dance with Kate Middleton—I mean, come on, she's a princess. And you know what? Every time people ask me questions like this, I wind up dancing with the person. So, Kate, I'll see you soon.

What three words would you use to describe yourself?

Passionate, energetic, blond.

ACKNOWLEDGMENTS

To my family—my mother for carrying me nine months and for introducing me to this world with love. You have always been my cheerleader and such a believer—not just a believer in me, but in everyone who has crossed your path. My father: for being the most consistent man I've known. You taught me what unconditional love is. You have shown me through your example how to never waver in my morals and beliefs. To all my sisters—Sharee for being Mom #2 while we were growing up, and for actually bearing six other kids so I have the privilege of being an uncle to them. Thank you for being the first one of the Hough kids to take ballet and lead the way for me to take dance classes! Marabeth: In the past few years, you've figured it all out. You've been an incredible example of how to choose a happy life and live it to its fullest. Thank you for showing me what I sound like when I talk to people. We make perfect sense to each other, even though no one else understands what we say! Katherine: Thank you for being the light in our family. You light up a room, and you always lead the way in having a great time and bringing so much joy and laughter to us all. As Dad would say, "You're my Face of America, too." Jules: Thank you for always being there and for being my partner in crime on this crazy adventure. Your drive and your passion are always inspiring to me. You're not only an amazing sister—you're one of my best friends. To all the Hough and Heaton clan: thank you for the incredible memories. A special thank-you goes out to Grandma and Grandpa Hough for giving us a place in Coeur d'Alene to come together as a family and reconnect and build more memories each and every year.

To my extended family—Shirley, Corky, Mark, and Nan. Shirley: You taught me to have a strong work ethic and you've been an incomparable example of what one can achieve through dedication and hard work. You've been an unwavering support in my life. I know I can always count on you and it means everything to me. Corky: You have inspired me from the time I was a kid. You took me into your home and treated me as your second son. You showed me what passion is—the name of our house was *Live with Passion*—and you taught me through example to follow my dreams no matter how crazy they seem. Nanny: You were our absolute life support. Words can't describe how much you took care of us. Thank you for all our late-night chats. You never let me eat alone. Mark: Thank you for being the brother I never had and for sharing your parents with me. You truly have become a vital and influential part of my life, and I look forward to being the best man at your wedding someday.

To all of my teachers and mentors for putting me on the right course and taking the time to share your thoughts and experiences. You challenged me, pushed me, and saw potential in me. Rick Robinson: you made dance cool. To the gang at Center Stage: thank you for creating a nurturing and exciting environment that made me want to continue on my path. Thanks to Italia Conti and all of my teachers and administrators, especially Anne Sheward. Thank you for not giving me too much of a hard time for skipping a few classes! I appreciate all your support.

To all of my partners over the years on *DWTS*—Jennie Garth, Shannon Elizabeth, Brooke Burke, Lil' Kim, Joanna Krupa, Nicole Scherzinger, Jennifer Grey, Ricki Lake, Maria Menounos, Shawn Johnson, Kellie Pickler, Amber Riley, and Amy Purdy. Each and every one of you has taught me something invaluable about women and myself! A special thank-you to Kellie for writing the foreword, and to Ricki for going through her phone and sharing pictures of us in action. Also, a shout-out to Amy Purdy who, during the course of writing this book, has helped me reaffirm everything I want to do and be. You've brought out the best in me and remind me why I do what I do.

To my *DWTS* family—all the pros, judges, and producers for giving me the most incredible six years of my life.

Thanks to my team: Rob Weisbach, Susan Madore, Max Stubblefield, and Jeff Golenberg. You guys go above and beyond. My writer, Sheryl Berk, for working around my crazy schedule and putting it all together; the gang at HarperCollins—Lisa Sharkey, Amy Bendell, and Paige Hazzan for allowing me this great opportunity to put my thoughts and experiences to paper.